Itinerant Philosophy
On Alphonso Lingis

ITINERANT PHILOSOPHY

ON ALPHONSO LINGIS

edited by Bobby George & Tom Sparrow

punctum books ✴ brooklyn, ny

 ITINERANT PHILOSOPHY: ON ALPHONSO LINGIS
© Bobby George & Tom Sparrow.

http://creativecommons.org/licenses/by-nc-nd/3.0

This work is Open Access, which means that you are free to copy, distribute, display, and perform the work as long as you clearly attribute the work to the authors, that you do not use this work for commercial gain in any form whatsoever, and that you in no way alter, transform, or build upon the work outside of its normal use in academic scholarship without express permission of the author and the publisher of this volume. For any reuse or distribution, you must make clear to others the license terms of this work.

First published in 2014 by
punctum books
Brooklyn, New York
http://punctumbooks.com

punctum books is an open-access independent publisher dedicated to radically creative modes of intellectual inquiry and writing across a whimsical para-humanities assemblage. punctum indicates thought that pierces and disturbs the wednesdayish, business-as-usual protocols of both the generic university studium and its individual cells or holding tanks. We offer spaces for the imporphans of your thought and pen, an ale-serving church for little vagabonds. We also take in strays.

ISBN-13: 978-0692253397
ISBN-10: 0692253394

Facing-page drawing by Heather Masciandaro.

Table of Contents

Note to the Reader	1
Dorothea Lasky Love Poem: After Alphonso Lingis	3
Bobby George and Tom Sparrow Interview with Lingis	7
Jeff Barbeau Early Notes Toward an Ontology of Fetishes	21
Timothy Morton Objects in Mirror Are Closer Than They Appear	37
Alphonso Lingis Doubles	61

John Protevi
    Alterity and Life in the Thought of Lingis   69

David Karnos
    Personal Correspondences   81

Joff Peter Norman Bradley
    Becoming-Troglodyte   111

Jeffrey Nealon
    On *The Community of Those Who Have Nothing in Common*   129

Dorothea Olkowski
    What is an Imperative?   143

Jonas Skačkauskas
    Interview with Lingis   149

Graham Harman
    On *Violence and Splendor*   169

Note to the Reader

In 2012 we launched the now-inoperative journal *Singularum*, whose *modus operandi* read like this:

> *Singularum* operates on the premise that every facet of life yields transformative aesthetic encounters. It provides an independent venue for theorizing, transmitting, and staging these encounters. Its strategic aim is to exhibit thinking born at the interface of aesthetics & pedagogy.

Unable to sustain this short-lived project in its original form, we decided to convert its two volumes into books, the first of which is devoted to the work of nomadic American philosopher Alphonso Lingis. Thanks to the generosity of punctum books director Eileen Joy, along with her dedicated accomplice Andrew Doty, you are now reading the foreword to what was once Volume 1 of *Singularum*.

Tom Sparrow & Bobby George
Pittsburgh, Pennsylvania & Sioux Falls, South Dakota
July 2014

Love Poem: After Alphonso Lingis

by Dorothea Lasky

What I to you
I loved you
But you also meant nothing to me

You were nothing but
A box jellyfish
The edges always coming out to meet the water

A skin of water, not water-blue
So that there was nothing we could find like ourselves

And nothing like a center
So that the animal was not a beak
But a movement forward

So that speech was not a thing to say
But a thing to be attracted to
What silly songs we did find then

Itinerant Philosophy

And when I went swimming through the pond
I was a transparent body
That went to you

And when I went flying through the air
It was your distinction, not similarity
That called to me

And when I died and my awe
Completely upturned
I held myself, my breath

My spiritus
Which had always swirled around you
In clear folds I knew of, the skin

So that the only indication
Of another world
Were the rain and snow

And when I was reborn again
I was only an infant
But still, you asked me to dance with you

And I did dance with you, my father
Do you remember us both, both babies
Moving closely around the sky

In the icy wind
In the orange water
Full of flies

In the sunny terrain
Of black hills
The home

Lasky: Love Poem

The home we knew
And even if it takes a while
I will meet you there again

Interview with Alphonso Lingis

conducted by Bobby George & Tom Sparrow

BG & TS: As you know, we're planning to enter your body of work through the lens of photography and geography. We thought we'd start our conversation there, at that conjunction. What motivated you to start to include photos in your text?

AL: In *Excesses* I thought I had to show a temple at Khajuraho, for readers who had never seen images of them. I also wanted to include a Nuba man photographed by Leni Riefenstahl—a photograph that, when I first came upon it, made me decide to go there (the text does not explain that).

The photographs are not inserted at places in the text that they would illustrate; they are put before the chapters. They bring readers to the places and people that the texts will describe and discuss.

When in 2009 I went back over 40 years of photographs to pick out those that were published in *Contact*, I was astonished and moved to find that I remembered every one of those people, so many only encountered for a few minutes on the street—and remembered the place, the time of day, the circumstances where I encountered them, the words we exchanged. It made me realize that the photographs show not simply a particular individual, but a setting, a field or arena where events took place. As Leni Riefenstahl's photograph had sent me to East Africa, the other photographs in the book send readers to places far away and now long ago.

The images are in their own way narrative—and the texts in their own way depict. In recent decades so many philosophers have denounced the idea that language is representation. They have not analyzed the way language lays out a setting of the world, makes us see people and events. We speak of absent things, far-off things and things that have passed on, and language depicts them and makes them continuous with the environment visible about us.

BG & TS: In a way, it seems to us that philosophy has not always taken photography seriously, at least not seriously enough. Not unlike language, philosophy has denounced photography as representation. Yet, your texts and photos announce a 'setting, a field or arena', at once intimate and distant, moving beyond these criticisms. Can you articulate this oscillation between language and photography, and how you see the expansion into a new geography?

AL: Thinking about photographic images, I think we come to revise the way philosophy distinguished between reality and image and between subjective and objective. Discover images that the things, and not the human mind, engender.

Since Descartes and Locke and their friends, a critical question for philosophy was: How can I be sure that I am not dreaming? How to establish the difference between perceptions that genuinely exhibit real things, and dreams that are concocted within the mind by the mind? "Images" in general were taken to be fabricated by the mind itself.

I instead set out to recognize that the things themselves engender "images" or doubles of themselves—shadows, halos, the images of themselves they project on water, on the glass of windows—and also on the surfaces of the eyes of mammals, birds, fish. For example, the puddle of water that appears shimmering on the surface of the road ahead in a hot day is not "subjective," produced by the mind; it is engendered by the road and the sun and everybody in the car sees it.

I then was really struck by the fact that these real or objective images the things generate captivate us and excite in us the pleasure of seeing. For Heidegger we are always on the lookout for implements, obstacles, paths, objectives. To the contrary, I recognized that when we step out into the world we are captivated by the shifting profiles and angles the things exhibit, the shadows and the reflections, the glitter on the lake and the radiance blazoning the outlines of the clouds, the shifting shadows and light on the face on the person we are talking to. And all this excites pleasure and keeps us fascinated and delighted by the things arrayed about us.

Merleau-Ponty distinguished between the "real properties of things"—the shape and size and color when we are in the optimal viewing position and all the "perspectival deformations" which we take as relays toward that vision of the real shape, size, and color.

But I think that all these perspectival variations, shadows, reflections swarm in the environment about us, and we do not only take them as transitions toward the sight of the real shape, size, and color. They captivate us in themselves, delight us, excite pleasure.

It is true that the mind can also fabricate images—in dreams, daydreaming, "imagination." So I distinguish:

—the appearances in which things reveal their real shape, size, color to us stationed at the optimal position and right lighting.

—the appearances that we take as transitional toward those real appearances. For example, seeing the table as rectangular even though we are looking at it from an angle.

—the perspectival variations, shadows, reflections, etc. the things themselves engender.

—images that are fabricated within the mind by the mind. These can be simple, false, or creative, artistry.

Photographic images are made by light and the camera; the photographer only positions and focuses. But the pleasure of photographic images is to capture images that the things themselves engender, in certain lighting, in shadow, in specific ways they group together.

Thinking about language and photographic images also leads to new conceptions of both. The concept of representation is obscure and misleading. Words do not simply stand for, stand in the place of, things that are absent. They do not simply stimulate our minds to produce images of things. I was very struck by Heidegger's statements about how words invoke and summon forth things. (I think of the words of the medium who summons the dead to appear in the room.) When he speaks of the bridge over the river Rhine, we do not simply attend to an image or concept of the bridge in our own minds; instead we attend to the bridge itself where it is, on the Rhine. The words of a novel lay out a landscape, a situation, events about us. (We do not simply look at the words and imagine the object each word refers to.) (Nor do the words simply direct attention to a landscape we have already imagined.) With the words that name the protagonist and some details of the setting, the whole protagonist and the complex setting form about us. Last summer I read Knut Hansun's *Growth of the Soil*. Written in a spare, economic language. But as I read the book how present and how dense and complex life in the Norwegian landscape in the last century hovered about me.

In looking at photos I took 40 years ago, I trembled to realize how it all became present again in the image—the shy or ironic feeling of the person, the density of life in that person, the spot on the road one day in India, the rhythm and sounds of that day—all those reflections and images radiating off the person, the road, the things of the setting. That is how I came to recognize a kinship between language and photography—that power in both to invoke and summon forth, bring things into presence.

You ask about the new geography language and photographs unfold, a wonderful and striking thought. I am afraid I have gotten involved in the "ontological status" of images and of the vocative power of language. But I shall stop now; I shall have to ponder your question more.

BG & TS: Certainly the photographs in your texts recall scenes that are, for you, autobiographical. The affective content of these images must be much thicker for you than it is for your readers, although your words often work to generate a rhythm that is capable of drawing readers into the photograph and the scene it is borne out of, thus providing a certain tangibility to your prose. Levinas, in "Reality and Its Shadow," speaks of how the musicality and rhythm of images has the capacity to render the spectator a passive participant in the spectacle itself. As a photographer, do you see yourself as spectator or participant in the rhythm of your photographs? Whatever your view, do you find that your photographs have the ability to convey to readers the autobiographical content of your travels?

AL: I will not talk about the experience of professional photographers, those who produce wedding albums, architecture and landscape books, mesmerizing images for celebrities and commodities. I just want to talk about walking when one walks with a camera.

I had long resisted buying a camera, thinking that there was something false about collecting images of things seen and people encountered and who have passed on, trying to retain the past. I thought that what was real was what from a trip left one changed. I started taking pictures when a friend who was taking me to the airport gave me a camera on the way.

I soon realized that the camera had changed my perception. The light: it was no longer just cleared space in which things took form; it had direction, it led the gaze, its shafts excavated situations isolated in the dark, sometimes it spread in a scintillating, dazzling, blazing medium without boundaries. Shadows took on substance; they stretched, flowed, condensed things in themselves. It occurred to me that I saw them that way when I was a child. Things looked different: the contours of shadows and of things that overlapped other things pushed out the contours that contained things in themselves. Flat surfaces showed corrugations, grain, stubble and texture, and sheets of gleam. And the continuity of the landscape drifting by would be abruptly broken by momentary events—the spiraling neck of a heron probing the space, the poised pause of an antelope, the legs of a child in an arabesque she will never be able to do once grown up, the grin of a passerby at something inward. The landscape is abruptly splintered, a segment isolates, magnetizes, and pulls the glance into it.

A gesture, some steps, a contour, an encounter stops passing, stops transitioning, and breaks out, presents itself. A profile turned, an overlapping of wagon and wall, a gleam or zigzag line of light, most often only there an instant. But disconnected from the field, from situations passing, from orientations and goals. Purely present.

Abruptly you stop. That gait, that stride that kept your body going on arrested, that sweep of the eyes braked, your breath stopped, your heart beat skips. Redirected, you are pulled into that disconnected segment where a strange light glimmers, a bird bobs his head, a smile flashes. You feel that tense poised pose of an antelope contracted in your body, that smile flashing in the face of a stranger in the road fills all space and flashes in your eyes.

This transfiguration of the environment into scintillating moments of pure presence, and these moments of ecstatic participation, are the reason to walk with a camera. To be sure these moments of rapture in the midst of forest trees all around, in the midst of a crowded street happen without a camera in one's hand. They are the reason our eyes are not, as Heidegger would have it, always interested, on the lookout, looking for objectives, paths, implements, obstacles. Our eyes are fascinated by the immensities outside, never tire of looking, because of these disconnected moments of surprise and pleasure, of rapture.

But with the camera in hand, these trance moments become metaphysical; the sinewy movement of a branch on the surface of a lake is doubled, displaced, into your eyes and heartbeat and also across the camera into far-off places and rooms where it will dance again in a long vanished light. A camera, one could say, is a tool or an instrument. But when you install a light switch, it is all lined up first in the mind: the wire that will conduct the current to the interruptor, the wire that will bring the current to the ceiling light, the wire that send the current on, the wire that will bring excess charge to the ground, the insulated pliers that will twist and connect the wires. With a camera one never did understand the process, the chemical compounds on the film, the digital breakdown of the image. And unlike the hand that wields a chisel or that aims a rifle, the hand that raises the camera and touches the button does not become skilled. With a camera decades ago, there was some manipulation; one had to check the light meter, to set the speed and the focus; now the camera does everything.

And then you wait to see the result. The camera will do things the eyes did not: it will flatten the landscape, crowd in adjacent things the eyes had kept back, enlarge the outstretched hands. A stroke of chance presented the enchanting fragment and the moment; now a stroke of chance produces the image of it in different scaffolding. By chance enchanted, or trivialized. You discard or delete 95%, 99% of the images.

There was the moment of enchantment, of trance; the camera only recorded it (transformed, perhaps wretched). But the photo image retains its bond with the fragment or event that once became pure presence. We look at the image of our godmother, immigrant from the old country, standing in a field of high grass holding us when we were a six-months-old baby, and we are transported back to that field and the warm bosom of that woman long dead. We look at the image of our grandfather, scrawny youth in his uniform, who never returned from the Great War, and we are transported to a place we never have been. Looking over photographs one has taken over the decades, the years of one's life are transformed into hundreds, thousands, of disconnected momentary trances. They are gifts the world gave. They are gifts to give others. You go back a few days later to give her that photograph you took of the street vendor; she calls her children, her mother, you laughing take photos of them to give them a few days later. In a far-off land you give your friends, the rascally grin a street kid in Calcutta gave you and them, the colors a frog in Madagascar gave to the heavenly light.

BG & TS: Mesmerized, inspired, and enchanted by the depth of your response. It reminds us of experimentation, and childhood innocence and exploration, both a call to Heraclitus and a new path forward for philosophy.

In a way, Orson Welles revealed a new cartography, and new possibilities for thought, with his search for time. With the introduction of depth of field, Welles explored these layers and recesses, experimenting with the adventures of life that comprise our immanence.

Not yet knowing what was possible, Welles pioneered a cinema of time, a new geography, or ethics and aesthetics of affects. As Deleuze called it, Welles constructed, or revealed, "a little piece of time in its pure state". Paul Klee, perhaps, had something like this in mind, when he suggested we take a line for a walk, and this is precisely where we locate your unique philosophical expressions.

As a philosopher, as a traveler on a line of experimentation, taking a camera for a journey, exploring fields and terrains for philosophical inquiries, or searches, what role do you see education, or pedagogical guidance, playing in this adventure? Which is to say, do your adventures have pedagogical effects?

AL: The terms "education" or "pedagogy" never signified much to me, even in the classroom, where I selected books that gave me illumination and excitement and shared them with young people, regularly receiving, with gratitude, insights from them.

I first thought about gratitude some thirty-five years ago, in France. Gratitude is an action. Giving thanks. When someone arrives with a bottle of wine, we look at its color in the candlelight, savor its perfume, pour it into our best glasses, pour it to all our guests before we fill our glass. When someone gives us a gift, we do not just put it on a shelf and sit down to talk about whatever. We receive the gift, it takes time, we take it in both hands, take it in with our eyes, turn it about, contemplate its features. And we show it, share it with others.

Easter week on the Côte d'Azur, the year that I was teaching at the Université de Nice. Chris had taken a break from her studies and had come to spend two weeks with me. Nice was filled with thousands of especially Parisians who had come to escape the dreary end of the Parisian winter on the Mediterranean coast. But, quite untypically, it was raining here, steady, unending rain day after day, and the Parisians were gloomily drinking bottle after bottle of wine in the cafés and restaurants. I had an old VW bug and I said to Chris: "Why fight it? Let's go up into the rain!" We put on coats with parkas and got into the car. Chris's guitar was in the back seat. We headed into the Maritime Alps that rise abruptly to ice-covered summits behind the city. I was driving at random, just going up, and at a certain moment noticed a dirt road and drove up it. After some twenty minutes it ended at a stone wall some twelve feet high over which we saw some rooftops. "It's a fortified village," I said. "It must date from the sixteenth century when the Mediterranean was patrolled by Saracen pirates." We got out of the car; the rain had diminished to a misty drizzle. We found the gate in the wall; inside there were some twenty stone houses. Here and there, there were breaks in the roofs where the tiles had been blown off and broken. "It's deserted!" Chris exclaimed. We wandered down the lanes and came upon a chapel; we were able to push open the door.

Inside, on one wall there were naïve frescos. We were silenced, and Chris seated herself on the floor facing the simple stone altar.

After awhile I walked outside and wandered to where the terrain was highest. Black clouds were rolling over the ice-covered mountain peaks and furling down between them like ink dropped into water. From time to time there were bolts of lightning that blazed across the ice sheets. Then I looked down, and far below a break in the clouds had opened a shaft of light under which the Mediterranean blue sparkled silver. My body standing there felt awkward, unworthy of the grandiose heights, and instinctually settled to the ground. My eyes gazed quietly into the distances, and from time to time my body shifted into one or other of the simple yoga asanas that I had learned. My mind was emptied of everything but the black clouds and the glaciers.

George and Sparrow: Interview with Alphonso Lingis

After perhaps an hour or so I got up and wandered down the lanes of the village. On the other end of the village I came upon Chris, seated on a rock softly and intently playing her guitar. We had separately realized what grandiose gift our eyes had been given, and felt the need to do something to receive it, something modestly worthy of it.

When it was dark we drove back down in silence. Back in my apartment, we made sandwiches and opened a bottle of wine. After, Chris took up her guitar again, and I heard her strumming like she had played on the mountain. I wanted to write about this scene which was, I thought, the most grandiose my eyes had been given to see. I wrote about it to a friend. As I wrote I saw the words were making the scene more intense to me and settling it deeper into my heart. My letter took a long time, with many crossings-out and rephrasings. I realized that I could not share the event on the mountains unless I had written as well as I could, written better than any lecture on a philosophical text that I had prepared that year.

It was then that I realized that thought—which is about data, about some things or events that are given, which comprehends, takes in, what is given, ponders it, feels its weight, and produces words that are understandable and open to others, that exist for others—thought is gratitude.

I was in a shikara, a kind of gondola, in Dal Lake in Kashmir, as the day came to a close. It was my first trip to India, and also the first time I had a camera. I was shy about photographing people, thinking it intrusive and objectifying. As the boat moved by I had turned my camera to the row of willow trees trailing down along the shore. Then suddenly I saw in my viewfinder that there were men bathing in the river. Embarrassed, I pushed the camera down and looked up. But they had seen me, and were waving and shouting "Thank you!" I was puzzled, and eventually thought that they were grateful for being taken worthy of photographs. That a foreigner had come from afar and instead of photographing palaces was photographing poor people. A few days later I developed the roll and went to give the men their photos. After that I set out to give everyone the photos I had taken of them. It was usually easy to find them again: poor people are going to be there when you go back, or people who know them are. If I was leaving the next day, I could often find someone in the area who could write and give me addresses. People were visibly delighted when I returned with the photos; they would treasure photos they could not afford of their parents, children, grandparents. I ended up taking fewer pictures of buildings and landscapes and more and more pictures of people met at random. I came to experience taking photos as essentially giving of gifts.

I never took slides. I disliked the idea of seating people in my house and projecting slides of my trip for them, determining how long they would have to look at each image. I mounted the best pictures in albums; friends would take down whatever they liked and view the images as they liked. Something to give them pleasure, to give them access to faraway places, to give them the trust and tact of people from far away. When I started putting some photographs in the books I published, it was in the same sentiment of offering discreet gifts to people I will never meet or hear from.

BG & TS: In terms of photography, do you prefer wide-angle lenses, or do you achieve this strange familiarity and connectedness through an array of telephoto shots? What we mean to express is, there is a great sense of humanity in your photographs, a suspension of judgement, and an exhilaration of intimacy. How do you achieve this level of trust? In many respects, Annie Leibovitz managed to capture this closeness that we feel in your work, as she photographed her dying lover, Susan Sontag.

George and Sparrow: Interview with Alphonso Lingis

AL: Trust is taking what is not known as though it were known. Every relationship is based on trust, since we do not see the intentions, feelings, and motivations of another. With someone we have known a long time, or investigated his past, we take a number of past behaviors as indication of his future and present intentions. But the chance that he or she may say or do something different is what makes our encounters with others fascinating.

There is nothing more exhilarating than trusting someone of whom one has no past acquaintance, no social contract, no language in common.

When you walk alone in foreign lands, people who glance at you are tempted to trust. Because of the intrinsic fascination and exhilaration of trust.

Of course walking alone is to go disarmed and disarming. Trust elicits trust. The trust that is visible when they stop and look at you in the face elicits trust in you. And responding without wariness or reserve elicits trust in them.

To really respond to the other involves tact. Tact is the light touch that docs not seize hold or manipulate or possess. It is letting the other be and act in his or her space. It is also sensitivity; it is to let the other affect one, with his or her curiosity, affection, probings and reserve. In tact one senses something of the other's desires and pleasures.

Trust is not a matter of photographic techniques. It begins by asking permission.

Some Early Notes Toward an Ontology of Fetishes

by Jeffrey Barbeau

We now need an ontology of fetishes, a fetishist ontology of things. The substances of things are not simply outside us, outside the sphere of human consciousness, and they are not only relations of causal determinism between them and the human mind. Things, in the structures and substances, attract us and inspire us and direct us and organize our movements, order us.[1]

—Alphonso Lingis

Itinerant Philosophy

For the past eight months I have been involved in an art project in which I take a photograph of a moment that typifies the general feeling of my day. I envisioned this project as a way to take this ongoing and often ineffable process of typifaction and make it slightly more observable. What this has amounted to is a very loose and necessarily imprecise record of the emotional tone of my life for the past two hundred days or so. My plan is to continue with this project for the next two years. An even 730 days. What I hope to achieve is a productive coupling of practical obsession and virtual resignation.

What I have gleaned from this series of two hundred photographs is not so much a predictable series of images that follows one from the next, but more like a record of subtle and not so subtle experiential undulations. Not testaments to a resilient and self-identical presence, but rather continuous self-differentiation. If photography has long been a tool for the biopolitical regulation of life—of documenting identity—I am currently interested in the capacity of the photographic image to explore the novel qualities of duration. Following

Alphonso Lingis, this is not the record of a sovereign and self-legislating subject, but an account of life as we contend and actualize ourselves from within the materiality of things, vibrations that register on our bodies, rhythms that entice us. It is, in short, an openness to the strangeness around and in us. For Lingis,

> The ceaseless activity of the mind to fix concepts and meanings on things appears as an anxious compulsion to staunch the leakage of strangeness. The sense of strangeness is not a cognitive recognition; it is the experience of the collapse of cognition, or vertigo, throbbing in raw emotional intensity.[2]

To my mind, this project is not a matter of the simple aestheticization of experience. Experience, as I have learned, is aesthetic from the very start: as subjects we are co-constituted and emerge as such through our engagement with an eventful and sensual field of encounters. Our purview as particular subjects (as students and researchers and artistic producers, for instance) is generated from the continual productivity of sensual forces, temporary stabilizations, minor modifications, and bouts of real volatility. As Lingis suggests,

> A working artist is not one who has an encyclopedic appreciation of artworks but one who has a passionate devotion to materials and forms that speak singularly to him or her. An artwork emerging in his hands captivates the artist and guides his hand; it goes beyond or goes outside whatever meaning that artist has conceived for it. It beckons him toward unknown paths. Are not artworks so many scattered sites outside the domain of work and reason, in the realm of chance?[3]

In my capacity as a researcher and an artist, I have found continual inspiration and creative gumption through a subjection of my thinking to this 'realm of chance.' What is more, I am constantly intrigued by the role that visual and material culture can play in an exploration of this insurmountable quality of 'strangeness' in our lives. All of the photographs included herein are meant to witness our mostly mundane, and occasionally exorbitant, emergence from an inexhaustible realm of beings and things that both engage and exceed our selves. I consider it a modest, tentative contribution to a visual cultural 'ontology of fetishes,' a survey of our immersion in both built and natural environments.

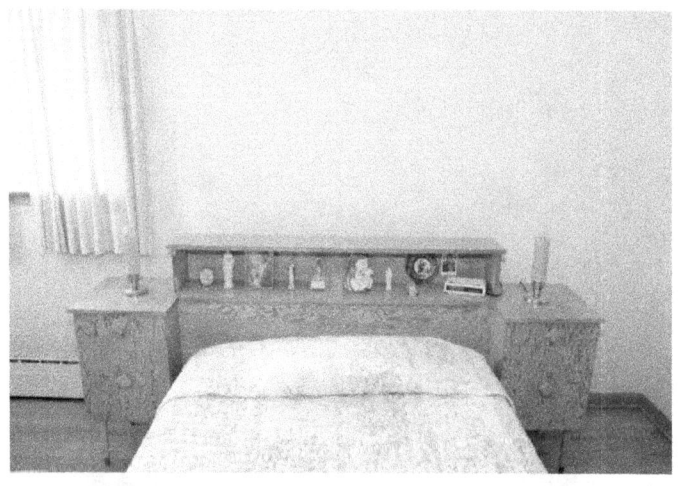

[1] Alphonso Lingis, "Towards An Ontology of Fetishes: An Interview with Alphonso Lingis," *Cultural Politics* 5.1 (2009): 115.
[2] Alphonso Lingis, "Strange Emotions in Contemporary Theory," *Symploke* 18.1–2 (2010): 7.
[3] Alphonso Lingis, "The Voices of Things," *Senses & Society* 4.3 (2009): 279–280.

Itinerant Philosophy

Barbeau: An Ontology of Fetishes

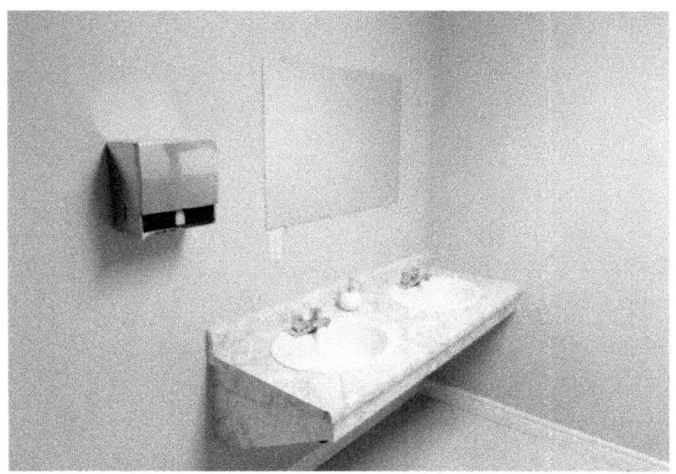

Itinerant Philosophy

Barbeau: An Ontology of Fetishes

Itinerant Philosophy

Barbeau: An Ontology of Fetishes

Itinerant Philosophy

Barbeau: An Ontology of Fetishes

Itinerant Philosophy

Barbeau: An Ontology of Fetishes

Objects in Mirror Are Closer than They Appear

by Timothy Morton

AESTHETICS

Yukultji Napangati's painting *Untitled* (2011) is in the Art Gallery of New South Wales, and was highly commended for the 2011 Wynne Prize. The painting is reproduced here [Fig. 1], but the image simply fails to do it justice. The first one seems to evoke it better. But this is one of those images one must see in the flesh.

At a distance it looks like a woven mat of reeds or slender stalks, yellowed, sun baked, resting on top of some darker, warmer depth. A generous, relaxed, precise, careful yet giving, caring lineation made of small blobby dots. The warmth reminds you of Klee. The lines recall Bridget Riley. As you come closer and begin to face the image it begins to play, to scintillate, to disturb the field of vision. It oscillates and ripples, more intense than Riley. How did I know this was a woman artist before I found out who it was? In fact this is a painting about, a map of, a writing about, a line of women traveling through the sandhills of Yunala in Western

Australia, performing rituals and collecting bush foods as they went. The painting is a two-dimensional map of an event unfolding a higher dimensional phase space.

Figure 1: Yukultji Napangati, *Untitled* (2011).

Then something begins. What? You begin to see the "interobjective" space in which your optic nerve is entangled with the objects in the painting.[1] The painting begins to paint right in front of you, paint the space between your eyes and the canvas. Layers of perception co-created by the painting and the field of vision begin to detach themselves from the canvas in front of you, floating closer to you. This "floating closer" effect is one I associate with the phenomenology of uncanniness. The experience you have in a strange place, or a strangely familiar place evokes the feeling: objects in mirror are closer than they appear.

The painting gazes. It appears to extrude itself out of the canvas towards your face. It does not offer itself up for inspection or penetration, like a perspective painting. Instead, Napangati's painting strafes the viewer like a scanner or an X-ray machine. It is an unnerving experience, being seen by a painting. When I saw it, all the hairs on my arms and my friend's arms stood up, as if they too were caught in some crisscrossing electromagnetic field. The painting watches you: it does not allow you to form an attitude towards it. In this sense, it is almost the absolute opposite of conceptual art. You are not permitted to form concepts of any kind. The work is more akin to a sircn or a warning light than a picture-of-something. It beeps at you, scanning you.

Intersecting shards of patterns within patterns, patterns across patterns, patterns floating on top of patterns. A constant mutagenic dance between the levels of patterns. The painting is a device for opening this phenomenal display. It comes lurching towards you, hypnotizing you and owning you with its directives of sandhill, women, rituals, bush food, walking, singing, lines. You feel gripped by the throat with the passion of the imagery. All the hairs on your arms stand up and the painting has you in its electromagnetic field. The painting dreams. Causality begins.

What does this mean? I do not access Napangati's painting across a space. Rather, the painting appears to abolish the supposed distance between itself and me. The image is not a mute object waiting to have its meaning supplied by a subject, nor is it a blank screen, nor is it something objectively present "in" space. Rather the painting emits something like electromagnetic waves, in whose force field I find myself. The painting forcefully demonstrates what is already the case: space and time are emergent properties of objects.

The fact that this fact is common to relativity and to phenomenology should give us pause. Perhaps just as remarkable is the fact that relativity and phenomenology arose roughly synchronously towards the beginning of the twentieth century. Just as Einstein discovered spacetime was the warped and rippling gravitational field of an object, so Husserl discovered that consciousness was not simply an empty limpid medium in which ideas float. Consciousness, as revealed by phenomenology, is also a dense, rippling entity in its own right, like the wavering water of Monet's contemporary water lily paintings: the water that is the true subject of those paintings.

The paintings to which we have grown accustomed presume a disembodied subject floating in a void, capable of imparting meaning to objectively present things. A perspective painting, for instance, contains implicit instructions for viewing, a place from which the painting will render the most "lifelike" three-dimensional illusion. The work of the painting as such is supposed to vanish without a trace, leaving the illusion suspended in front of us for our inspection. Modernist art attempts to shatter this illusion. But Napangati's painting is not in the illusion making or illusion shattering business whatsoever. Pleasing and shocking (thus pleasing in a higher key) the bourgeoisie is not on its agenda in any sense. The painting destroys the distance necessary for the aesthetic illusion to function, yes. But it does not try to abandon the aesthetic dimension: far from it. Instead, it takes that dimensional all the more seriously. In order to render the illusion of a three-dimensional space from which the trace of painterly labor has vanished, there has already to be a play, a dance of some kind, some sort of phenomenal display, like the stage set that enables the actors to strut around. Napangati shows us the wiring underneath the normal aesthetic artifact, so to speak, but *this wiring is also part of the aesthetic.*

Causality

The aesthetic form of an object is where the causal properties of the object reside. Theories of physical causation frequently want to police aesthetic phenomena, reducing causality to the clunking or clicking of solid things.[2] It is not the case that a shadow is only an aesthetic entity, a flimsy ghost without effects. Plato saw shadows as dangerous precisely because they do have a causal influence.[3] When my shadow intersects with the light-sensitive diode, the nightlight switches on.[4] When a quantum is measured, it means that another quantum has intersected with it, altering it, changing its position or momentum.[5] Aesthetics, perception, causality, are all almost synonyms.

When the diode detects my shadow, it perceives in every meaningful sense, if we only accept that objects exert an aesthetic influence on one another (*aisthenesthai*, Greek "to perceive"). When I am caught in another's gaze, I am already the object of causal influences. Causality does not take place "in" a space that has been established already. Instead, it radiates from objects. The gaze emanates from the force field of a Yukultji Napangati painting. It gathers me into its disturbing, phantasmal unfolding of zigzagging lines and oscillating patches.

Doesn't this tell us something about the aesthetic dimension, why philosophers have often found it to be a realm of evil? The aesthetic dimension is a place of illusions, yet they are real illusions. If you knew for sure that they were just illusions, then there would be no problem. But, as Jacques Lacan writes, "What constitutes pretense is that, in the end, you don't know whether it's pretense or not."[6] Intense yet tricksterish, the aesthetic dimension floats in front of objects, like a group of disturbing clowns in an Expressionist painting. If there are only objects, if time and space and, as I'm arguing here, or rather gently suggesting, not even so much as stating yet, just beginning to evoke, to tune in to the possibility that causality is like time and space an emergent property of objects—if all these things float in front of objects in what is called the aesthetic dimension, in a non-temporal, nonlocal space that is not in some beyond but right here, in your face—then nothing is going to tell us categorically what counts as real and what counts as unreal. Without space, without environment, without world, objects and their sensual effects crowd together like leering figures in some Expressionist masquerade.

From this point of view, causality is wholly an *aesthetic* phenomenon, involving induction, transduction, seduction, whatever-duction. These events are not limited to interactions between humans or between humans and painted canvases or between humans and sentences in dramas. They happen when a saw bites into a fresh piece of plywood. They happen when a worm oozes out of some wet soil. They happen when a massive object emits gravity waves. When you make or study art you are not exploring some kind of candy on the surface of a machine. You are studying causality. *The aesthetic dimension is the causal dimension.*

Art is important because it's a direct exploration of causality. Post-Newtonian physics involves a lot more than just little metal balls clunking one another. Nonlocality, for instance, is the fact (a highly repeatable fact, at this point) that two particles, seemingly separate, can instantly affect one another in some sense.[7] Entities interact in a *sensual ether* that is (at least to some extent) nonlocal and nontemporal.[8] That's how objects can influence one another despite the fact that they withdraw from all forms of access. So when old fashioned art criticism speaks of timeless beauty, it is saying something quite profound about the nature of causation, not about spuriously universal human values.

Consider mechanist theories of causation. Machine-like functioning, which is what our common prejudice often takes causality to be (at least since Newton and Descartes), must only be one specific kind of emergent property of some deeper nonlocal, nontemporal ocean in which things directly are other things. Machines are made of separate parts, parts that are external to one another by definition. What causality *just isn't* is this kind of mechanical functioning, like the metal balls in an executive toy. The click of the balls as they hit one another is a sound that implies the existence of at least one other object—the ambient air that vibrates, causing the click to be heard. How come this click or clunk is more real than other forms of causality such as attraction, repulsion, magnetism, seduction, destruction, and entanglement?

Clunk causality implies a determinist view: two balls must be contiguous with one another, the causality only goes in one direction, and there must be at least a necessary, if not a sufficient reason for the clunk in the ball that does the clunking. Yet when we go down a few levels, we discover that quantum behavior is irreducibly probabilistic. What does that mean? It means that indeterminacy is hard wired into the behavior: it's not as if we could clean up our way of analyzing it and it would then look determined. So there are physical reasons why determinism doesn't work: we're talking about both sufficient *and* necessary conditions failing at some point. It means that Hume is in trouble.[9] But there's another big reason not to like determinism. When you have a probabalistic fact such as the likelihood that you will get cancer if you smoke, and you are a determinist, you can wish that fact away.

This is what tobacco companies do. There is no "proven link" between smoking and cancer—but *that's evidently not the point*. Likewise, global warming denial takes a leaf out of the determinist notebook. Since there is no obvious link between the rain falling on my head and global warming, it must be untrue. *Or the theory of causality given here is distorted.* Large complex systems require causality theories that are non-deterministic just like very small quantum scale ones. Clunking is an illusion that seems to happen to medium-sized objects such as billiard balls, but only when we isolate the clunk amidst a welter of other phenomena.

The Arabic philosopher Al-Kindi defines all causes as *metaphorical*—apart from God, the unmoved mover, (Al-Kindi is an Aristotelian theist).[10] Al-Kindi did so when my ancestors were clunking one another (talking of clunks) with crudely fashioned weapons, in the last years of the tenth century AD. Causation is metaphorical—that means that causes are overdetermined. The balls are held in place by a wire frame. The frame sits on a desk. The desk is part of an office in a large corporation. All these entities are causes of the executive toy's clunking sounds. Overdetermination, metaphor—they mean the same thing. Or, in translation, *translation*: *metaphor* is just Greek for *translation*, since *meta* means across and *-phor* means *carrying*. This is a far more suitable way to think causality than mechanical clunking. It provides a reason why many forms of empirically observed causation are probabilistic.

Aesthetic-causal nonlocality and nontemporality should not be surprising features of the Universe. Forget quantum physics: even electromagnetic fields and gravity waves are nonlocal to some extent. At this moment, gravity waves from the beginning of the Universe are traversing your body. Maxwell and others who pioneered the notion of electromagnetism imagined the Universe as an immense ocean of electromagnetic waves. And then of course there's the real nonlocal deal—the quantum mechanical one. This is when the aesthetic shape of an object is what a fruit fly smells (a quantum signature), not the volatile molecules themselves. Or consider the aesthetic shape of an electromagnetic field (how birds navigate, using tiny quantum magnets in their eyes).[11] Since at this level matter just is information, theoretical physics is already in an aesthetic kind of a conceptual space. Even the atomist Lucretius imagined causality working through aesthetic "films" emitted by objects.[12] But of course the arguments here go beyond a fanciful exploration of theoretical physics. They can be applied to any sort of entity whatsoever, not just the kind the physicists study.

One substantial advantage of arguing that causality is aesthetic is that it allows us to consider what we call consciousness alongside what we call things and stuff. The basic quantum level phenomenon of action at a distance happens all the time. Think of a black hole. Are there any in the vicinity? Yet somehow you are linked to them. Bertrand Russell denies physical action at a distance, arguing that causation can only be about contiguous things. If there is any action at a distance, he argues, then there must be some intervening entities that transmit the causality.[13] Yet isn't this an elegant definition of the aesthetic dimension? Action at a distance happens all the time if causation is aesthetic. What is called consciousness just is action at a distance. Indeed, we could go so far as to say that consciousness-of anything is action at a distance. Empirical phenomena such as mirror neurons and entanglement bear this out. Minimally, action at a distance is just the existence-for-the-other of the sensual qualities of any entity.

In Plato's time they used to call action at a distance *demonic*. That is, it was the action of demonic forces that mediated between the physical and nonphysical realms of existence. This is what Socrates says about art in *Ion*: he compares art to a magnet in a string of magnets, from the

Muse, goddess of inspiration, to the artist, to the work to the performer, to the audience and so on, all magnets linked by some demonic force.[14] Nowadays we call this demonic force electromagnetism, but really it's remarkably similar to Plato's insight: the electromagnetic wave transmits information over a distance; a receiver amplifies the information into music coming through the speakers of the PA system. In an age of ecological awareness we will come again to think of art as a demonic force, carrying information from the beyond, that is, from nonhuman entities such as global warming, wind, water, sunlight and radiation. From coral bleaching in the ocean to the circling vortex of plastic bags in the mid Atlantic.

Now we should not think that this "sensual ether" is some kind of adhesive that glues pre-existing "subjects" and "objects" together. Nor should we imagine that it is a restaurant in which subject and object might finally hit it off. Subject and object will never hit it off, for the simple fact that the concepts subject and object are prepackaged ontic contraband, imported from the long history of ontology.[15] Such a "between" would indeed be a version of "aesthetic ideology": an attempt to reconcile the ugly divorce between subject and object.[16] Against such an aestheticization, however, we would be right to insist that the aesthetic is crucial to understanding causality. We must therefore distinguish rigorously between the *aesthetic* and *aestheticization*.[17]

Aestheticization is just the conceptual imposition of aesthetic concepts onto prepackaged subjects and objects. The aesthetic however, is nonconceptual and cannot be packaged in this way. Its atemporal nonlocality should already have warned against this. If we don't wish to load the dice in favor of a particular kind of being (say *Da-sein*, say the human) we are left with a simple solution. The aesthetic dimension is simply *the interior of some object*: this is how objects are able to encounter one another. When I reach for the phone, I do so on the interior of a room. When I reach for the phone, I do so on the interior of a solar system. When I reach for the phone, I do so on the interior of a universe. The "sensual ether," then, is not like the ether of pre-Einstein physics at all, or the supposed Higgs field of quantum theory's Standard Model. Such entities allow objects to float around, have mass, and so on. If we were thinking of a physical ether, a quick glance at Locke's devastating assault on the idea of an "ambient fluid" that contains all the other entities will set us straight.[18] Such a physical ether must be composed of ether particles, argues Locke: and in what fluid are they floating?

If, by contrast, the causal "ether" is simply the way one entity "dreams" itself or another one, it is constituted by these entities as such. When I reach for the phone, I don't imagine myself as an objective subject trying to grasp an objective object, like Wile E. Coyote in *Roadrunner*. Still less do I need to imagine myself reaching through a space "between" prepackaged me and the prepackaged phone. This might happen, but only after the phone has gripped me, alarming me with its piercing ring or with the thought of some person I must call, or seducing my laziness, pulling me away from the essay I have to write. In Shakespeare's *Twelfth Night*, Olivia says, "The clock upbraids me with the waste of time."[19] Olivia doesn't think to look at the clock: the clock looks at her. This is what Alphonso Lingis calls *the imperative*, which we can detect in the way objects demand to be handled in specific ways.[20]

WHAT IS THE DIFFERENCE BETWEEN A DUCK?

There is no such thing as a phenomenologically empty space. Space is teeming with waves, particles, magnetic seductions, erotic curvature, and menacing grins. Even when they are isolated from all external influences, objects seem to breathe with a strange life. A tiny metal tuning fork thirty microns long rests in a vacuum. To the naked eyes of the observers outside, it is breathing: it seems to occupy two places at the same time.[21] There is already a rift between an object and its aesthetic appearance, a rift within the object itself. Causality is not something that happens between objects, like some coming out party or freely chosen bargain into which things enter. It pours constantly from a single object itself, from the chorismos between its essence and its appearance.

An object is therefore both itself and not-itself, at the very same time. ("What is the difference between a duck? One of its legs is both the same.") If this were not the case, nothing could happen. The uncanniness of objects, even to themselves, is what makes them float, breathe, oscillate, threaten, seduce, rotate, cry, orgasm. Because objects are themselves and not-themselves, the logic that describes them must be paraconsistent or even fully dialetheic: that is, the logic must be able to accept that some contradictions are true.[22] Objects are dangerous, not only to themselves, but even to thinking, if it cleaves to rigid consistency. If thinking refuses to accept that objects can be dialetheic, it risks reproducing the dualisms of subject and object, substance and accidence, that are unable to explain the most basic ontological decision—the one that insists that things are objectively present, as they are. The thing becomes imprisoned in a philosophically constructed cage, a mechanism, or in some kind of ideality that falsely resolves the dilemma by shunting everything into a (human) subject. Moreover, thinking itself becomes brittle. The more rigorous the metalanguage, the more susceptible it is to more and more virulent contradictions.[23] Thinking should learn from *Antigone* and bend, like a willow: "Seest thou, beside the wintry torrent's course, how the trees that yield to it save every twig, while the stiff-necked perish root and branch?"[24]

Phenomenology, then, is an essential cognitive task of confronting the threat that things pose in their very being.

Without it, thinking is unable to break through the traditional ways of philosophizing that Heidegger calls "sclerotic."[25] After phenomenology, we can only conclude that a great deal of philosophizing is not an abstract description or dispassionate accounting, however adequate these may be, but only an intellectual defense against the threatening intimacy of things. Moreover, since there is very little difference between what happens to a light sensitive diode and what happens to a human when they encounter a shadow, we can only conclude that there is a strange kind of nonhuman phenomenology, or, as Ian Bogost puts it, an *alien phenomenology*.[26]

Things can dream one another because they are always already not themselves. Not even the thing itself can objectify itself. The mud is capable of receiving the dinosaur footprint. If it were totally its muddy self in a noncontradictory way, it would be opaque, permanent, impervious, "objective." Causality happens because a dance of nonidentity is taking place on the ontological inside of a thing. The mud muddies: it dreams about the dinosaur in its muddy, mud-pomorphic way. Napangati's painting "paintings" me. It doesn't remain in perfect isolation, but sends out dreams of itself that intercept me as I walk towards it across the gallery floor.

I do not encounter patterns and relations that are resolved in my mind into paintings, mud, and glasses. These things encounter me directly, as themselves. But more precisely, every entity throws shadows of itself into the interobjective space, carving out its own version of Plato's cave. It is like the poem by Gerard Manley Hopkins:

> As kingfishers catch fire, dragonflies draw flame;
> As tumbled over rim in roundy wells
> Stones ring; like each tucked string tells, each hung bell's
> Bow swung finds tongue to fling out broad its name;
> Each mortal thing does one thing and the same:

Deals out that being indoors each one dwells;
Selves—goes itself; *myself* it speaks and spells,
Crying, *What I do is me: for that I came.*[27]

What Lingis notices, however, is that this *myself* has an uncanny dimension. Like the person who assures you they are being sincere, can we ever really believe that objects don't play tricks with us? Again: "What constitutes pretense is that, in the end, you don't know whether it's pretense or not."[28] Duns Scotus speaks of the *haecceity* of a thing, its *thisness*, and Hopkins translates this into verse.[29] Yet the thisness is not imposed from without, objectively. It wells up from within. Hopkins himself says so explicitly: *What I do is me*. Quite so: it is a case of *I* versus *me*. In this difference between a reflexive and a nonreflexive personal pronoun, we detect archaeological evidence of the rift between a thing and its appearance. What Hopkins gives us then, if it is a rendering of the real, is not a brightly colored diorama of animated plastic, but a weird stage set from which things stage their unique version of the Liar: "This sentence is false." To speak otherwise is to have decided in advance what things are, which contradicts the way the poem itself forces us to experience things. "Tumbled over rim in roundy wells / Stones" are felt and heard before we hear what they have to say for themselves against the walls of the well and in the deep water within: the first line is an invisibly hyphenated adjective, tumbled-over-rim-in-roundy-wells. The adjective takes almost as long to read as it might take for an average stone to hit the water. The adjective draws out the stone, just as the dragonflies "draw flame." The stone becomes its tumbling, its falling-into-the-well, the moment at which it is thrown over the rim. Then splash—it's a stone all right, but we already sensed it as a non-stone.

The very notion of movement involves the paradox that a thing is "at once" p and not-p ($p \land \neg p$). If we want to avoid

Zeno's paradox, we have to be ready to accept that a tumbling stone both is and is not "here." If we don't do this, the stone will never reach the bottom, because we will be able to take smaller and smaller slices of objectified "time" thought as a "between in which" the stone sits, now consistently here, now consistently there.[30] Motion is not something that an object "does" on occasion: motion is a deep ontological feature of a thing. Thus Napangati's painting can "move" while it hangs motionless on the wall; indeed it can "move me" in the affective sense for the very same reason. Motion is never a matter of billiard balls rolled across a preexisting surface of "space" or "time," but instead motion arises from the rift between a thing and itself, between its *I* and its *me*. Motion betrays the clownlike strangeness of a thing.

ETHICS

When I experience beauty, I resonate with an object. The object and I attune to one another. Kant describes beauty as a tuning process. "Beautiful" is what I say to myself when an impersonal, "object-like" cognitive state arises that seems to emanate from the object itself. It is as if the object and I are locked together in inseparable union.

The beautiful object fits me like a glove. Kantian beauty, however, is unlike Aristotelian and Horatian decorum.[31] Decorum provides objective rules, an external, systematic set of criteria for what counts as beautiful, a checklist. Kantian beauty, by contrast, is a symptom of a major discovery of something nonobjective. Kant thinks this discovery as the transcendental subject, but object-oriented ontology thinks the discovery as the withdrawal of objects. In other words, what Kant discovers about human beings—that part of their nature is sealed from empirical access—applies to nonhumans. Because of the rift between essence and appearance—which must not (again) be associated with the supposed difference between "substance" and "accidents"—any entity whatsoever has this hidden property. There is evidence for this even in Kant himself, as the following should show.

Something in the beauty experience is hidden from me, even while I am experiencing it. Beauty is nonconceptual. It involves a certain "je ne sais quoi." Nothing in the object directly explains it: not the parts, because this would be sheer positivistic reductionism; not the whole, because that would be another kind of reduction (the parts are now expendable). Yet beauty seems to emanate from this thing. Just this particular, unique thing, is the locus of beauty. Everyone in their right mind should find it beautiful, I think, yet if I were to impose this on others, it would ruin the experience. I know my particular experience of beauty is not shared, but I know that you know what beauty is. A certain unconditional freedom opens up, along with a certain coexistence without content. No wonder Kant considered the experience of beauty to be an essential part of democracy. Beauty is an event in being, a sort of gap, a gentle slit. Beauty allows for a cognitive state that is noncoercive and profoundly nonviolent. The master of this realm is Theodor Adorno, whose meditations on Kantian beauty are unsurpassed at this time.[32]

But what are the conditions of possibility for the experience of beauty to occur? What, as it were, are the phenomenological physics of beauty? As we explore these conditions we uncover a remarkable body of work. The name of this body of work is Alphonso Lingis. It is in the mode of Lingis that I have been writing this essay. We may now be in a position to see with some clarity the very special place that aesthetic events have in the philosophy of Lingis.

Kantian beauty tacitly presupposes a being that can be wounded by colors, sounds, smells, textures and tastes: affected by them, so as to resonate such that the tuning process of beauty can commence. This is not simply a realm of mere appetite, as Kant suggests, because that would reproduce a difference between humans and nonhumans (animals, for instance) that is untenable and problematic.[33] Moreover, in appetite I roam like a hungry wolf over the carcass of things—it seems as if powerful objects at the very least suspend this aggressive craving, always already suspend it be-fore the event of beauty takes hold. And stranger still, as Lacan noted well, there is a symmetry between Kantian beauty and sadism, a cold lust concerning an infinitely opaque object.[34] Before the gentle slit of beauty is made, then, the knife must be ready and the arm must be in range. It is this dimension, a dangerous and uncanny dimension of "levels" and "directives," that the thinking of Lingis addresses.

What is called *aesthetic distance*, then, is a misnomer for a nonconceptual *aesthetic intimacy* in which habitual patterns, taken as objective fact, are suspended. This suspension does not occur around or above things, but rather it emanates from the very heart of things. The thing is a suspension of itself: the *I* and *me* of a thing. Aesthetic distance is not "between" an object and another object, or between a subject and an object, but rather it lies between a thing and itself ("What is the difference between a duck?"). It would be better to describe the "distance between" as an aestheticized distance that has nothing to do with primordial aesthetics, the carnival of Liars ("This sentence is false").

In a car crash, in an ugly divorce, time seems suspended, slow motion. Only afterwards do I start to piece together "what happened." Time as a regular sequence that acts as a neutral medium for events is a retroactive positing. The car crash, the divorce, is a primordially aesthetic event that *has no idea what it is* while it is happening. Trauma is not some empty gap or void within the smooth field of regularly functioning time.[35] Rather trauma is the irruption of a "more real," uncanny "undead" world of aesthetics as the scripted non-contradictions of "everyday life" shatter of their own accord. Trauma unmasks regularly functioning phantasms ("me," "my life") *as* phantasms. That is precisely why trauma is traumatic. It strips the world bare of the illusion that it isn't an illusion, and the accompanying illusion that illusions are just candy sprinkles on the surface of a noncontradictory cake.

The aesthetic-causal dimension, then, implies the irreducible coexistence of things. Things are coexistence in their being. Things, with all their gaps and inconsistencies, are enmeshed with one another. A wire mesh is a network of gaps and links. When I pump a bicycle tire, when I look at Napangati's painting, I am enmeshed in a series of interlinked emanations of beings. Because of this enmeshment, it is not possible to attain transcendental escape velocity from things: the very attempt takes place in the context of enmeshment. There is no way to peel the enmeshment off oneself, since it penetrates into the core of being: beings are self-contradictory, themselves and not-themselves. The mesh is viscous, as if the wires were made of honey: "The vicissitudes of this life are like drowning in a glass pond."[36] The very attempt to tear myself away enmeshes me further. Thus conscious coexistence with the mesh involves a form of nonviolence. At the very least, since every act tears at the mesh, and tears me, who is (in) the mesh, it would be best to refrain from harm. Translated by Lingis, Levinas quotes Pascal: "My place in the sun is the beginning of all usurpation."[37]

BEAUTY IS DEATH

"My place in the sun is the beginning of all usurpation": even my death is a wound to others, not confined to humans. Yet the beauty experience is also evidence that there is something in me that is not my ego. The beauty experience proves to me that there are others. What do we mean then when we say,

"It was so beautiful I almost died"? Is there more than metaphorical truth in this statement? Is beauty an experience of death, or near-death? Adorno writes that the shudder of beauty shatters the encapsulated subject.[38] When an opera singer sings just the right note, at just the right pitch and volume, the sound waves resonate with the wine glass in such a way as to destroy it. On slow motion film, we can see how just before it is destroyed, the glass undergoes a shudder, a sort of glass orgasm. The resonant frequency matches the glass perfectly.

From the perspective of the alien phenomenology of the glass itself, might this indeed be an "experience" of suddenly losing a sense of boundary? And isn't this what beauty is? In the event of beauty, a non-self part of my inner space seems to resonate in the colors on the wall, in the sounds pouring into my ears. Hugely amplified, might this resonance actually kill me? "A beautiful way to die"—to be destroyed by vibrations that removed myself from myself.

For beauty to work, then, there must already be a surface capable of receiving the wound. It seems that the knife of beauty is able to insert itself into the slit between an object's essence and its appearance. Beauty "works itself in" to the already existing rift between an object and that same object, the fact that objects are dialetheic, fork-tongued. This rift is an inconsistency in the object that enables the object to end. It can be thought of as a *hamartia* (Greek, "wound"), which is what Aristotle calls a tragic flaw. When an object is entirely sundered from its appearance, its *hamartia* gets the better of it: that is called *destruction* or *death*. When I disappear into a black hole, you see on the surface an image of me that slowly fades. When someone dies, they leave behind memories, objects that they have handled, wounds. When a realist novel ends, the frequency and duration of the action on the page synchronizes ever more tightly with the action in the chronological sequence of events: ashes to ashes.

The reader's heart beats faster as the police mount the staircase, only to find the stretched out body of Dorian Gray, and a picture of him into which a knife has been thrust.[39] A dead crow becomes the dust and trees that surround it. When a Dzogchen yogini dies, in one of the spaces between existences (the Bardo of Luminosity), it is said that she allows her being to dissolve into the Clear Light "like a child leaping into its mother's lap."[40] It is said that her being shatters like a vase and the space inside the vase merges with the space outside. Or she allows her body to disintegrate into rainbow light (Tibetan, *jalu*). From her point of view, is as if the body wants to dissolve in this way. Only fragile ego is preventing the inevitable from happening. Yet the fragile ego is what dies a little in the beauty experience. Beauty is a signal from the realm of death.

Beauty, then, is a nonviolent experience of near death, a warning that one is fragile, like everything else in the universe. Beauty is the shadow of the threat to objects, *the threat that is objects*. Objects as such carry an inner threat, because of the rift between essence and appearance. Beauty is the call of the vulnerable flesh and the fragile glass. This explains perhaps why beauty is associated with experiences of love, empathy and compassion, themes that preoccupy pre-Kantian theories of aesthetic affect such as Adam Smith, and that also preoccupy ethics based on the Buddhist view of anattman (no-self).[41] It is the reason why we can articulate an ethics of nonviolent coexistence based on beauty. This ethics cannot truly be grounded in the abstract, rather cold Kantian version of aesthetic experience, with its rigid anthropocentrism and sadistic shadow side. It must instead be founded in the project laid out by Alphonso Lingis, the project of coming as close as possible to our already shared, disturbing intimacy.

Let us return to the question of a flexible, willow-like thinking that would be able to move with the torrent of things without becoming brittle and breaking, snapped because of the *hamartia* of its very firmness, its attempt to remain consistent. Surely then this thinking, which almost dies every time it encounters something not itself, is in itself a beautiful thinking? Hegel wrote that thinking is the encounter with non-identity, and Adorno massively adumbrated Hegel's thought.[42] Like a Mother Theresa of beautiful souls, Adorno's plea for nonviolence is moving and soothing, but somehow it remains an advertisement, a sermon, a cry of the heart in a heartless world. Thinking needs to risk its sanity a little bit, to put itself in some danger, not endlessly postpone the plunge by talking about how much a plunge is needed. The time for wringing our hands on the edge of the abyss is over, because humans brought about the *Anthropocene*, a geological period of Earth history marked by the deposit of a thin layer of industrial carbon in Earth's crust since 1790, and likewise, before what is known as the Great Acceleration, a deposit of a layer of radioactive materials in Earth's crust since 1945. A certain kind of Marxist critique is now irrelevant. The world is too much with us, and when critique tries to wrench us out it only laments how stuck it is.

It is in phenomenology that the task of dwelling in non-identity on non-identity comes about. It is in Lingis, drawing on the richness of the phenomenological tradition, that the encounter with strangers becomes possible, the encounter that, coming close to death by tuning, "saves the Earth." Lingis thinks beautifully.

Editors' note: This chapter's title is identical to the introductory chapter of Timothy Morton's *Realist Magic*, published by Open Humanities Press in 2013. The content is not identical, however.

[1] I use this term to denote something similar to, but wider than, the traditional phenomenological concept of *intersubjectivity*. See Tim-

othy Morton, *Realist Magic: Objects, Ontology, Causality* (Ann Arbor: Open Humanities Press, 2013), 26, 34, 64, 67–72.

[2] Phil Dowe, *Physical Causation* (New York: Cambridge University Press, 2000), 17, 25, 59, 63–64.

[3] Plato, *The Republic* Book 7, http://classics.mit.edu/Plato/republic.8.vii.html.

[4] Contra Phil Dowe, in *Physical Causation*, 75–79.

[5] David Bohm, *Quantum Theory* (New York: Dover, 1989), 99–115.

[6] Jacques Lacan, *Le seminaire, Livre III: Les psychoses* (Paris: Editions de Seuil, 1981), 48.

[7] The most recent explication can be found in Anton Zeilinger, *Dance of the Photons: From Einstein to Quantum Teleportation* (New York: Farrar, Straus and Giroux, 2010), 45–55.

[8] The term is Graham Harman's in *Guerrilla Metaphysics: Phenomenology and the Carpentry of Things* (Chicago: Open Court, 2005), 33–44.

[9] Dowe, *Physical Causation*, 14–29.

[10] Al-Kindi, "The One True and Complete Agent and the Incomplete 'Metaphorical' Agent," in *Classical Arabic Philosophy: An Anthology of Sources*, trans. and intro. Jon McGinnis and David C. Reisman (Indianapolis: Hackett, 2007), 22–23.

[11] Erik M. Gauger et al., "Sustained Quantum Coherence and Entanglement in the Avian Compass," *Physical Review Letters* 106 (January 28, 2011): DOI 10.1103/PhysRevLett.106.040503.

[12] Lucretius, *On the Nature of Things*, trans. William Ellery Leonard 4.26–215, http://classics.mit.edu/Carus/nature_things.4.iv.html.

[13] Dowe, *Physical Causation*, 63.

[14] Plato, *Ion*, http://classics.mit.edu/Plato/ion.html.

[15] The case against this contraband has never been made any better since Martin Heidegger's devastating assault in *Being and Time*, trans. Joan Stambaugh (Albany: State University of New York Press, 1996). On the notion of the "between," see especially 124.

[16] Paul de Man, *Aesthetic Ideology*, trans. Andrzej Warminski (Minneapolis: University of Minnesota Press, 1996); Terry Eagleton, *The Ideology of the Aesthetic* (Oxford: Basil Blackwell, 1990), *passim*.

[17] Robert Kaufman, "Red Kant, or the Persistence of the Third *Critique* in Adorno and Jameson," *Critical Inquiry* 26 (Summer 2000): 682–724.

[18] John Locke, *An Essay Concerning Human Understanding*, trans. Peter H. Nidditch (Oxford: the Clarendon Press, 1975, 1979), II.23.23–24 (308–309).

[19] William Shakespeare, *Twelfth Night*, http://shakespeare.mit.edu/twelfth_night/full.html.

[20] Alphonso Lingis, *The Imperative* (Bloomington: Indiana University Press, 1998), 25–38.

[21] Aaron D. O'Connell, M. Hofheinz, M. Ansmann, Radoslaw C. Bialczak, M. Lenander, Erik Lucero, M. Neeley, D. Sank, H. Wang, M. Weides, J. Wenner, John M. Martinis, and A. N. Cleland, "Quantum Ground State and Single Phonon Control of a Mechanical Ground Resonator," *Nature* 464 (March 17, 2010): 697–703.

[22] See Graham Priest and Francesco Berto, "Dialetheism," *The Stanford Encyclopedia of Philosophy (Summer 2010 Edition)*, ed. Edward N. Zalta, http://plato.stanford.edu/archives/sum2010/entries/dialetheism/.

[23] Priest, *In Contradiction: A Study of the Transconsistent* (Oxford: Oxford University Press, 2006), 9–27.

[24] Haemon, in *Antigone*, trans. R.C. Jebb, http://classics.mit.edu/Sophocles/antigone.html.

[25] Heidegger, *Being and Time*, 20.

[26] Ian Bogost, *Alien Phenomenology, or What It's Like to Be a Thing* (Minneapolis: University of Minnesota Press, 2012).

[27] Gerard Manley Hopkins, *The Major Works*, ed. Catherine Phillips (Oxford: Oxford University Press, 2009).

[28] Lacan, *Le seminaire, Livre III*, 48.

[29] John Duns Scotus, *Philosophical Writings*, trans. Allan Wolter (Indianapolis: Hackett, 1987), 166–167.

[30] Priest, *In Contradiction*, 172–181.

[31] Horace, *On the Art of Poetry*, in Aristotle, Horace, and Longinus, *Classical Literary Criticism*, trans. T.S. Dorsch (Harmondsworth: Penguin, 1984), 82–83.

[32] Theodor Adorno, *Aesthetic Theory*, trans. and ed. Robert Hullot-Kentor (Minneapolis: University of Minnesota Press, 1997).
[33] Immanuel Kant, *Critique of Judgment: Including the First Introduction*, trans. Werner Pluhar (Indianapolis: Hackett, 1987), 45–46, 51–52.
[34] Jacques Lacan, "Kant with Sade," trans. James B. Swenson Jr., http://www.lacan.com/kantsade.htm.
[35] Trauma as gap is how Badiou theorizes the Event. See Alain Badiou, *Being and Event*, trans. Oliver Feltham (New York: Continuum, 2007).
[36] Chögyam Trungpa, "Instead of Americanism, Speak the English Language Properly," in *The Elocution Home Study Course* (Boulder: Vajradhatu, 1983).
[37] Emmanuel Levinas, *Totality and Infinity: An Essay on Exteriority*, trans. Alphonso Lingis (Pittsburgh: Duquesne University Press, 1969), 37–38. See also Levinas, Interview with François Piorié, in *Is It Righteous to Be? Interviews with Emmanuel Levinas*, ed. Jill Robbins (Stanford: Stanford University Press, 2001), 53 [23–83]. The Pascal quotation forms one of the epigraphs to Emmanuel Levinas, *Otherwise than Being: Or Beyond Essence*, trans. Alphonso Lingis (Pittsburgh: Duquesne University Press, 1998), vii.
[38] Adorno, *Aesthetic Theory*, 245–246, 331; see also 113, 281, 323–324, 346.
[39] Oscar Wilde, *The Picture of Dorian Gray*, ed. Robert Mighall (London: Penguin, 2003), 212–213.
[40] Padmasambhava, *The Tibetan Book of the Dead: The Great Liberation by Hearing in the Intermediate States*, trans. Gyurme Dorje, ed. Graham Coleman with Thupten Jinpa, introductory commentary by the Dalai Lama (New York: Viking, 2006), 176.
[41] Adam Smith, *The Theory of Moral Sentiments* (London: Penguin, 2010).
[42] Theodor Adorno, *Negative Dialectics*, trans. E.B. Ashton (New York: Continuum, 1973), 5–7, 12.

Doubles

by Alphonso Lingis

Willows, rocks, cascades, clouds, peregrines, dragonflies: real things. They are present, in the present. Having left them, we find them again. They are where they are, independent of us, whether we locate them or not. There are times when all our names, categories, and uses for them fade away, and we are confronted with their brute reality.[1] The urban and historical context of the Place de la Concorde fades away and we find ourselves standing on rough stones glistening in the rain.[2]

Evolutionary biology contests Platonic metaphysics and philosophical idealism: our perception of our environment is not essentially different from the perception of other biological species. Fish, birds, and mammals survive because the things they perceive are indeed external to their minds, independent of them, and as real as they are.

Things turn to us one side of themselves at a time. But as we stand before an armchair and shift position, this side of it tilts up another side and indicates sides to come. To see a real thing, and not a fixed surface pattern, is to see it as a cohesive and coherent whole existing in depth and across duration.

We see the front plane of the refrigerator and see its solidity extending down the sides and across the back.

Things are present before us with their pasts and futures. A rock retains the shape given it centuries ago by water freezing and melting; a tree trunk retains the swerve it took decades ago to distance itself from the shade of the adjacent tree. Its growth in good season and bad can be seen in the rings of its trunk. A corpse retains the expression of resignation or pain the body felt at the last movements of its life.

The wall that is green was green and will be green; a spread of green that would be there only an instant would lack the substantiality of a real thing. The garden bench emerges from its past and its substantiality shows its future. Descending the canyon, we see its shapes cut by the water and the wind that are even now wearing away the path under our feet.

As we walk we see the continually elongating, widening, and narrowing sides and stretching or shrinking patterns each thing turns to us. As the shifting of the cloud far beyond our reach can hold our rapt gaze, so our eyes, without surveying, without any practical concern, are absorbed by the changing facets of a building, by the turns and swirls of a pine as we walk up the hill.

The reality of things is not confined within their contours. A rock compresses the earth below it and is supported in its place by the earth. Under the sun it radiates heat and light about itself. A bush crumbles the earth with its roots and emits gases into the atmosphere. An abrupt discharge of electricity in the storm clouds emits a thunderclap that shatters a goblet in the dining room.

※ ※ ※

Things also engender doubles of themselves. Rocks and fences cast shadows on the ground, trees across the sidewalk, the crests of snowdrifts and sand dunes shadow the troughs. The brook sends streaks of light downs the reeds and the willows. The reeds and the willows flick reflections of themselves into the water and into the translucent globes of the eyes of herons, deer, and humans.

The colors of things bleed out of them to tint or tarnish the atmosphere. The shapes of things merge into one another to form waves and swells and compressions. The buildings radiate their wood or stone tones upon one another and into the light and the air, making the atmosphere of one town different from another. In twilight the colors of the forest disengage from the contours of the leaves and dissolve the branches in a miasma of fermenting greens. The metal chains and jewels of the matrons in the benefit dinner link up with the glitter of the glasses and gleam of the silver. The colors of a face do not only outline the surfaces and pores of the carpentry of that face, but also interact with one another in the brew of a sensual, swarthy, or porcelain complexion. Yasunari Kawabata contemplates the strobe dabs of sulphurous glow from fireflies on the cheeks and brow of a woman in the night garden.[3]

Aural images of things move off them. The fruit rolling down the roof sends a run of rumble across the ceiling. In the bamboo thicket canes flick long thin shrieks into the wind. The water splashing over rocks in the brook sends a syncopation of sputterings over its banks. The fallen leaves send on with the breeze the whirr of their slidings and raspings. The sonorous images of things, their cracklings, thumpings, and thuds link up to form rustlings, rolls, or din. The splash of the raindrops echo in the splashes of raindrops all about to compose sizzle.

Many of these emanations are ephemeral while the things are enduring, but others endure after the things have passed on or passed away. The grass retains the imprint of the deer's body after it has left; the shale holds the shape of the dinosaur whose body has long decomposed.

Things react to these doubles; the moss flourishes in the shadow of the building, the grass lifts itself out of the imprint of the deer's body. Things react to their own doubles: bushes raise their flowers above their shadows.

* * *

Things cast doubles of themselves upon the surfaces of our bodies and upon our sensory surfaces. They cast reflections of their colors and shapes upon our eyes, send their reverberations into our ears, from a distance spread their tang and sweetness into our nose and mouth. And things cast the doubles that other things cast on their surfaces upon our sensory surfaces. The pond casts the zigzags of sunlight upon our eyes; the snow relays upon us the gesticulating shadows of the leafless trees.

Our bodies, like other things, cast shadows on the ground, send their reflections on the surface of the pond and the window and on photographic film, radiate their colors onto other things and into the light and the air. They also cast doubles of themselves upon the sensory surfaces of other bodies.

Our bodies also generate doubles of themselves that they leave in the past and project into the future. They leave imprints of their shape on the bed, on the beach, on photographic paper. They project doubles of themselves in the dance floor at the end of the drive, on the guests awaiting them at the wedding feast.

Our bodies also shadow themselves, have a double perception of themselves. Our eyes see, our hands touch little of ourselves. But as we sit, walk, reach for and manipulate things, a postural schema takes form in our bodies, holding our parts and limbs together, and giving us an inner sense of where and how our arms and legs are positioned. It gives us an inner sense of how our legs are extended under the table and how our hands are extended groping in the dark. We also have a "body-image": as we sit or walk or reach for things, we have a quasi-visual image of how our bodies look from the outside. It is not an "image" our mind is imagining; it is a perceptual sense of how our body looks as it would be seen from a viewing distance outside, which is generated by our postural schema. Like a reflection or a shadow cast by our postural schema.

Martin Heidegger argued that perception is intrinsically practical; we look about in order to get somewhere and do something; we perceive things by moving among them and manipulating them. But that is surely wrong: when we sit on the deck or walk to the store, we see and hear leaves fluttering to the ground, tree branches zigzagging across one another, birds careening in the sky, clouds drifting, wind gusting, crickets chirping, patterns, rhythms, tonalities, reverberations, mists, glows, glimmers, sparkles that we are nowise manipulating or using, nowise looking at them in view of doing something to them or with them. All that—lures and ensnares the eyes.

When captivated by the realm of shadows, reflections, reverberations, the I is but a semblance of its active self. It no longer focuses, disengages objects and objectives, and launches initiatives. Our eyes and our bodies are moved by the rhythm of the reflections of the trees and the clouds swaying on the surface of the lake. As the plane descends, we watch the lights of the city spreading across the dark below. We arrive at the concert hall, find our seat, survey the audience for people we know or know about, look at the musicians tuning up, appraise the conductor striding to the podium. Then the music begins, the sounds detach themselves entirely from the substances whose metallic or wood or catgut nature they revealed, are set free in another dimension where they link up in rhythms and melodies. Our freedom is bound, caught up in those rhythms and melodies; we follow the music like and with anyone about us. But involvement in a rhythm produces an intense sense of presence, an obsessed lucidity quite different from the obscurity and indistinctness in which habits, reflexes, or instinct operate.

We feel contentment when the substance of things fills a lack or need, a hunger or thirst. We feel satisfaction when the things do not obstruct, but lend themselves to our manipulations. But so much of our pleasure in the world, pleasure in being in the world, is a pleasure in the glows, gleams, and halos about things, in the reflections and shadows things cast about themselves. Our gaze skips and sways with them, attracted and delighted by them.

These doubles the things generate can also be disquieting and threatening. The oversized shadow on the window of an intruder. As twilight advances, the shadows advance over things, finally engulfing them, but we sense that in the night the sonority of the things intensifies and spreads far from them while they close in upon us, touch us without being seen.

* * *

Artists take up and prolong the fascination of our eyes and ears not with the "properties" of things, the shapes and colors that are stabilized in their integrated and subsistent structures, but with the shadows, reflections, auras, and mirages the things engender. Photographers capture the mists harboring a valley, the light blazing in the hair about a face. Music captures in the resonances and movements of sound forces that move us, that we receive in emotions.

In our lives, in our actions, what we do is ordered—by the paths and the obstacles, by the tasks, by the people about us, by the hungry horses in the barn, by the rivers and the forests, by the sun and the night. There are imperatives, injunctions, directives, prohibitions in the things about us. Enlightenment philosophy championed political freedom, from tyranny and oppression, and subsequent philosophy came to identify freedom with the very essence of humans.[4] But effective action is ordered by the possibilities and prohibitions that the things and the setting contains.

The shadows, reflections, halos, and reverberations of things also appeal to us, summon us, and order us. The sparkle of the dewy morning summons us outdoors. The shadows of the forest trees invite our footsteps and our rest. The luminous waves and runs of light in the coral sea orders our pleasured submission as we move into it and under it. The tone and atmosphere of the Zen temple imposes quiet and contemplation. Kawabata writes of the sound of the mountain that guided his itineraries, his ascents and his returns.[5] The rumble of the waves in the night orders our heartbeat and respiration as we sink to sleep at night. The cries of the fledgling bird fallen from the nest appeals to us. The rumble of the avalanche prohibits our advance.

---

[1] Jean-Paul Sartre, *Nausea*, trans. Lloyd Alexander (New York: New Directions, 1969), 127–131.
[2] Maurice Merleau-Ponty, *Phenomenology of Perception*, trans. Colin Smith (London: Routledge, 1962), 293.
[3] Yasunari Kawabata, *The Lake*, trans. Reiko Tsukimura (Tokyo: Kondasha, 1974), 133ff.
[4] See still today Martin Heidegger, *The Essence of Human Freedom: An Introduction to Philosophy*, trans. Ted Sadler (New York: Continuum, 2002), and Jean-Paul Sartre, *Being and Nothingness*, trans. Hazel Barnes (New York: Washington Square Press, 1956), 559–711.
[5] Yasunari Kawabata, *The Sound of the Mountain*, trans. Edward G. Seidensticker (New York: Berkeley Medallion, 1970), 21ff.

Alterity and Life in the Thought of Alphonso Lingis

by John Protevi

This paper pays homage to Al Lingis's mastery of key figures in the transcendental, existential, and phenomenological traditions of philosophy. In the works of the 1980s, *Phenomenological Explanations* and *Deathbound Subjectivity* among them, Lingis displayed a supreme control in explicating the tradition, preparing for the breakthroughs that characterize the great works written in his own idiom.

In particular, we will trace two reductions, enabling us to see how Lingis identifies three levels of subjectivity. Beginning with the sensibility inherent to intentional consciousness, Lingis performs a "reduction to sensuality," identifying auto-affective consciousness. He then performs a "reduction to substantiality," identifying the condition for hetero-affective or commanded consciousness. So, from sensibility to sensuality, and from there to commanded subjection. Of course this is only the order of reasons, if we can put it like that, not the order of being, in which the imperative is primary.

We will complement our reading of how Lingis performs these reductions and identifies these levels of subjectivity with readings of Michel Henry and of Kant.

FREEDOM, LAW, SENSUALITY, AND SUBSTANTIALITY

"Intuition of Freedom, Intuition of Law," the last Chapter of *Phenomenological Explanations* (Lingis 1986), provides a fine introduction to the two reductions and three levels of subjectivity we mention above.

Lingis begins with the phenomenology of freedom in Sartre: its appearance in affectivity, as anxiety. Juxtaposed to this is the Kantian imperative, the "primary and irreducible givenness of law" (Lingis 1986: 103). The theoretical use of reason is commanded to represent a lawbound nature, commanded by the form of law itself, not by any sensible intuition. Further, practical reason is commanded to think itself free of natural mechanism, but that means freely bound to construct maxims that take the form of lawbound nature.

But, by returning to Sartre, we see how Kant's imperative to conceive practical reason in the form of lawbound nature falters once one takes into account the irreducibility of an embodied perspective: "once one sees the perspectival structure intrinsic to any cognitive as well as to any practical field, one understands the structural necessity of the perceptually inobservable observing body, of the unmanipulatable manipulator-body" (Lingis 1986: 105).

But Sartre cannot explain how positing goals can "activate the executive forces of the material body," a lacuna to which Lingis brings the corporeal schema and inextricability of action and perception of Merleau-Ponty to address (Lingis 1986: 106).

But having found the origin of action in the capacities of the lived body, what then of constraint, force, law, imperative? "One has to perceive things, has to perceive the world" (Lingis 1986: 107). Hence Lingis's pointed question: have

Sartre and Merleau-Ponty escaped describing pre-reflective experience on the model of reflective experience?

Here Lingis makes one of his signature moves. Let's call it the "sensual reduction." Calling on Levinas (although we will use Henry as our *point d'appui*), he writes, "there is consciousness that is not conscious of some thing. There is sensibility that is not prehension of a form. There is sensuality in our sensibility . . ." (Lingis 1986: 107).

The sensual reduction in turn brings Lingis to his second reduction: that of sensuality to substantiality: "The sensuous element is not schema but substance; it supports us, sustains us, is sustenance, its content contents us" (Lingis 1986: 108). Lingis stresses again and again in his work that the consciousness of sensuous substantiality is auto-affective, not intentional.

But such auto-affectivity—which cannot be seen as ecstatic reaching out, but as "being-in one's own substance"—doesn't let us escape imperatives: "action is demanded" (Lingis 1986: 109). And action is not just making up lacks felt in auto-affection. Action is not generated merely by hunger. Action takes place in a world. "Why? What is this imperative that makes our existence a being-in-the-world" (Lingis 1986: 109).

And here is the spot for the appearance of the other in Kant: "respect for the other is respect for the law that rules in another" (Lingis 1986: 110). Which is also the point of entry of Levinas, who challenges the Kantian imperative in its universality, changing it to singularity: "the force incumbent on me: an appeal that singles *me* out, a command that orders me" (Lingis 1986: 110; italics in original).

It's this imperative that founds the subject not as "subject of sensuous enjoyment" but as "subjected to an imperative." This is the subject of hetero-affectivity, the subject as constituted in subjection, in *assujettissement*: "the position of being an agent does not arise in the midst of sensuous enjoyment

.... We have argued that being-in-a-world ... presupposes subjection to an imperative" (Lingis 1986: 111).

Which is to say that we are commanded to be free: "the freedom of [the] agent is not given in a primitive intuition independent of the world or [independent] of the imperative that requires a world" (Lingis 1986: 112).

Although there are many nuances to be added, we can recognize many of the lines of thought characteristic in Lingis's work in this brief sketch.

FORECAST OF THE REMAINDER OF THE PAPER

At this point, I'd like to pick up on two points on the nexus of alterity and life in Lingis's thought. This will show the great precision and density of Lingis's thought by explicating at length what he distills into sentences:

1. The notion of the inaccessible other thought on the basis of pure auto-affectivity, in Michel Henry, as a counter-point to Lingis's notion of subjection, of hetero-affectivity as auto-affectivity broken by the appeal of the other.

2. Kant's description of the respect of the law in the other, as we see it in Lingis's reading, in "Images of Autarchy," Chapter 2 of *Deathbound Subjectivity* (Lingis 1989). This hetero-affectivity occurs in and as pain, as the thwarting of the life force.

MICHEL HENRY AND THE AUTO-AFFECTIVITY OF LIFE

In *Material Phenomenology* (2008), Henry insists that classical phenomenology aims at the transcendental conditions of possibility of manifestation or appearance, that is, *how* things appear (not *what* appears). For Henry, "classical" or "historical" phenomenology is based in the claim that things appear as constituted by intentional acts, what he will call being "thrown into the light of the world." Intentionality is thus a condition of possibility of appearance; in other words, intentionality is a transcendental feature of subjectivity. But is intentional, constituting, subjectivity—transcendental subjectivity—itself such an object? We risk an infinite regress with a positive answer: it seems that making intentional subjectivity into an object requires another subjectivity to whom that objectified subjectivity appears.

In *Material Phenomenology* Henry also subjects Husserl's treatment of self-awareness to a careful reading, concluding that Husserl fails to isolate the auto-affection" of life as the true way in which subjectivity manifests itself; this failure necessitates a new, "radical" phenomenology.

For Henry, "auto-affection" is the purely immanent feeling that living beings have of the concrete modes of their life. One of Henry's prime examples is pain: pain is revealed in and through its very passive givenness: there is no intentional object constitution in the experience of pain, just pain as a purely immanent experience of life revealing itself to itself: a self-manifestation or self-appearance. The emphasis is on the way the auto-affection of life is the self-manifestation of subjectivity; intersubjectivity, in turn, is rooted in a "shared pathos" of life. This is the point of contrast with Lingis's work, in which intersubjectivity is founded in hetero-affectivity, in the imperative issuing from the other.

Henry addresses intersubjectivity via a reading of the *Cartesian Meditations*. For Henry, Husserl's descriptions of the constituted ego, which is used as the basis for the "apperceptive transfer" with the alter ego (Henry 2008: 109), misses the "original" ego self-given in auto-affection (Henry 2008: 108). Rather than a "phenomenology of perception applied to the other" (Henry 2008: 114) we should recognize our "real experience" of the other is in terms of "a feeling of presence or absence, solitude, love, hate, resentment, boredom, forgiveness, exaltation, sorrow, joy, or wonder" (Henry 2008: 104).

The problem comes with the reduction to the sphere of ownness in *Cartesian Mediations* 5. Here Henry will oppose the ("true") transcendental Ego with the "constituted ego" that is the basis for Husserl's analysis (Henry 2008: 108). Here we see a "demotion of the original Ego to the rank of a psychophysical ego appearing in an objective form in the world of my sphere of belonging" (Henry 2008: 110). Now we must be careful to remember that for Henry "the light of the world" is his term for intentional constitution: the originality of self-manifestation is "deposed" in the reduction to the sphere of ownness. The elements of the sphere of ownness "are deposed in the sense that appearing, which is the basis of their being . . . is their appearing in this first world of ownness" (Henry 2008: 106).

Following the thesis of ontological monism, this "first world of ownness" is still a world for Henry; it presupposes yet forgets the non-worldly, non-appearing auto-affection of life. As a result of this demotion, "the worldly ego in the primordial sphere of ownness functions as the pivot of the pairing association with the body of the other" (Henry 2008: 110).

Henry claims that in focusing on the constituted ego Husserl also enacts a "demotion of the body" in which "the body is no longer the radically subjective and immanent "I can" that I am and that is identical to my ego" (Henry 2008: 110). The key thesis, again, is that constitution is not primary self-manifestation: "*It* [the constituted body] *is shown in ownness but not in itself*" (Henry 2008: 110; italics in original).

The fundamental problem for Henry is that Husserl does not examine the true reason why the other can never be presented, but only appresented. From the fact that "every subjectivity understood in its original way . . . escapes from every perceptual presentation" (Henry 2008: 112) we should not conclude, as do Levinas and Derrida, that the other is too much an other to be presented.

Rather, Henry will insist, "it is not because the alter ego is an alter [that it escapes perception]; it is because the other is an ego that I cannot perceive the other in itself" (Henry 2008: 112–113). That is because the true ego, the transcendental Ego that is the "Ipseity" of transcendental Life, can never "appear" in the "light of the world," but can only self-manifest in auto-affection.

KANT AND THE PAINFUL THWARTING OF THE LIFE-FORCE

In the *Critique of Judgment* ("General Comment on the Exposition of Aesthetic Reflective Judgments"), Kant distinguishes the purely mental "feeling of life" [*Lebensgefühl*] from physical "life forces" [*Lebenskräfte*] (Kant 1987: 274); upon this distinction rests the entire critique of aesthetic judgment, which must distinguish empirical or physical interest in an object's possible effects on our health (physical life forces) from aesthetic disinterestedness focusing on the pure mental stimulation (mental feeling of life) occasioned by the presentation of an object. We can contrast this duality with the unity described in *Critique of Practical Reason*, where "pleasure always affects one and the same life-force [*Lebenskraft*] which is manifested in the faculty of desire" (Kant 1956: 23).

The feeling of life is affected in all registers corresponding to our higher powers: judgment, understanding, and reason. In addition to the pleasures and pains associated with aesthetic judgments of the beautiful and the sublime, we also experience cognitive and practical feelings. We feel a cognitive pleasure in discovering a harmony of laws of nature with our cognitive power, since we can unify heterogeneous empirical laws of nature under principles (Kant 1987: Introduction, V, 184; Introduction, VI, 187).

Practical feeling, on the other hand, is twofold: we feel pain in the thwarting of the inclinations in the face of the moral law, but this very pain will produce respect for the moral law as a "positive feeling" (Kant 1956: Part I, Book I, Chapter III, 73–74). We will pursue the connection of pain and the moral law as it plays out in the Critique of Teleological Judgment.

The teleological judgment of nature's purpose feeds into Kant's thought of the organism, turning it towards a theo-bio-politics. While the cultural production of man's capacities for purposiveness is the ultimate purpose of nature here on earth (Kant 1987: ¶83, 431), the final purpose of nature, that in virtue of which nature is planned, can only exist outside nature, in man as moral subject (Kant 1987: ¶84, 435; ¶86, 443). The purposive intelligence that would have the possibility of man's morality as its final purpose in arranging natural order must be a moral God. Thus nature and freedom are finally related in the thought of a moral architect God, a "legislating sovereign in a moral kingdom of purposes," who guarantees that nature must at least cooperate with our moral action (Kant 1987: ¶86, 444).

The key to understanding this aspect of Kant's thought is to consider culture. We must distinguish the culture of skill from the culture of discipline while at the same time searching for the connection to *Gewalt* as force, violence, and authority. The culture of skill prepares our capacity to set ourselves purposes, while the culture of discipline is negative, consisting in the "liberation of the will from the despotism of desires" which "rivets us to certain natural things" necessary for our biological survival, that is, the furthering of our life forces (Kant 1987: ¶83, 432).

In the culture of skill we are riveted to pleasure; freedom comes only through self-chosen pain. Nature has given us our impulses so we would not "neglect or even injure our animal characteristics" (Kant 1987: ¶83, 432).

With the culture of discipline however, we can develop our freedom to "tighten or to slacken, to lengthen or to shorten" our impulses "as the purposes of reason require." In an interesting twist, the way to the rule of reason is prepared by the pleasure of fine arts and sciences, which "make great headway against the tyranny of man's propensity to the senses and so prepare him for a sovereignty in which reason alone is to dominate [*Herrschaft . . . in welcher die Vernunft allein Gewalt haben soll*]" (Kant 1987: ¶83, 433).

Those purposes of reason are the painful establishment of the moral law as the ground of action in a person, as we learn in the *Critique of Practical Reason*. The establishment of the moral law as ground of action, "by thwarting all our inclinations, must produce a feeling which can be called pain," while the moral law, as positive in itself, commands respect in "striking down, i.e., humiliating, self-conceit" (Kant 1956: Part I, Book I, Chapter III, 73).

The pain of humility must be self-chosen, as Kant makes clear in discussing humility, "a sublime mental attunement, namely voluntary subjection of ourselves to the pain of self-reprimand" (Kant 1987: ¶28, 264). Here we see the political affect of morality parallel that of the sublime: the violent, painful striking down of our natural body will rebound to reveal a supersensible vocation.

In his moral philosophy, Kant objects to the propensity to make our subjective grounds of choice into an objective determining ground of the will, self-love, a propensity that can even attempt to make our self-love into law, the condition Kant calls self-conceit. Respect for the moral law reasserts the proper role of the rational moral law as sole legislator of the kingdom of practical reason. Respect for the moral law is a disciplinarian that through sublimely painful self-humiliation prevents the revolution that would place self-love in charge.

Now whether or not the feeling of admiration for the

purely rational will and the feeling of respect for the moral law are ultimately pleasurable is a difficult question. Just like the indirect pleasure of the sublime, a certain pleasure at the prospect of rational self-governance is produced on the basis of the immediate effect of pain produced by the moral law's effect on inclination. However, focusing on these immediate effects, Kant writes in the *Critique of Practical Reason* that "respect is so far from being a feeling of pleasure that one only reluctantly gives way to it as regards a man" (that is, recognizing the morality of others is also painful to us) (Kant 1956: 77).

Whether or not the feeling is that of pleasure, the focus on the rule of reason and the painful stifling of inclination is clear. In other words, whether Kant's political affect of self-chosen pain, of sublime humility and the moral crushing of the inclinations, is ultimately hedonic is questionable, but that it is dolorous through and through is clear.

And here, of course, at the point linking pain and imperative, is where Lingis will call upon Nietzsche and joy, Nietzsche and the love of the world, as other affects. Let's leave that for discussion, though.

Conclusion

What have we seen in expanding upon these two themes: auto- and hetero-affectivity, and the pain of the moral law? The readings show, with regard to the nexus of alterity and life, the depth and density of Lingis's thought, which distills, without sacrificing precision, whole dimensions of the thought of great philosophers. This distillation provides to Lingis's works of the 1980s their unique power, affecting us from within by a challenge from without, moving us, changing our lives.

Henry, Michel. 2008. *Material Phenomenology*, trans. Scott Davidson. New York: Fordham University Press.

Kant, Immanuel. 1956. *Critique of Practical Reason*, trans. Lewis White Beck. Indianapolis: Bobbs-Merrill.

Kant, Immanuel. 1987. *Critique of Judgment*, trans. Werner Pluhar. Indianapolis: Hackett.

Lingis, Alphonso. 1986. *Phenomenological Explanations*. Dordrecht: Martinus Nijhoff.

Lingis, Alphonso. 1989. *Deathbound Subjectivity*. Bloomington: Indiana University Press.

PERSONAL CORRESPONDENCES

by Dave Karnos

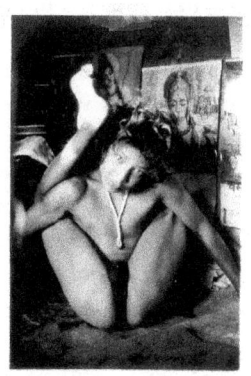

—What the shit is this? I never asked for this?
—Relax friend no need to read it!
—I will though take the moment to say I miss talking with you. And hope you get a job in the vicinity therefore.
  Namaste

Varanasi,
Kameswar Mandir
12-13

Thanksgiving, 2011

Dear Tom,

Three years have passed since you first asked me to write about Al Lingis and his correspondence with friends over the past forty years. Sixteen years have passed since Wolfgang Fuchs and I gathered together the first 20 years of Al's letters, with the intention of providing a sourcebook for researchers. *Letters from a Nomad Philosopher* (mss) compiled over 200 letters written between 1973 and 1995. Right now it sits on the floor before my fireplace, scattered around me in folders with headings like Flesh, Fun, and Friendship; on People and Philosophers; Birth and Death. It sits before me now much like the final exams that were spread around the floor in front of fish tanks and wall-to-wall bookshelves at Al's house in State College, 1972. As a graduate assistant for one of his big introductory classes, we were grading, holding pass or fail thumbs like the young Caesars we felt to be. Only then, as I recall clearly, when we would utter disgust at a piece and move it towards a would-be-fail pile, Al's hand would dart forward and intercept. A few quick searches and he would find a passage to read us, and surround its reading with evocations of tenderness, liveliness, loveliness, and looking up at us staring at him blankly utter something like "brilliant, don't you think?"

I have never forgotten that occasion. These utterances came as epiphanies to me—sudden and momentous hammer blows upon my way of thinking about things and people in terms of grades, of arrangements into piles, categories, and pigeon holes. To this day whenever I find myself before a situation calling for a sharp judgment, one usually bearing nasty outcomes, if I just pause enough a little voice will arise in my mind with a lovely refrain that dissembles any tension of the moment: "brilliant . . ."

Many others have been affected by Lingis over the years. Stellar observations can be found in the lovely homage compiled by Alex Hooke and Wolfgang Fuchs *Encounters with Alphonso Lingis* (Lanham, MD: Lexington Books, 2003). An exceptional take on his own books can be found in Mary Zournazi's interview with Lingis for Radio Eye in Australia (1999) [http://www.abc.net.au/rn/arts/radioeye/Foreign9.htm]:

> I don't think I have a policy statement on writing, but I do have some feelings. I have thought that the task of philosophical writing is to address yourself to some reality and for it to be in your own terms . . . I think I felt that very intensely the first time I went to India – when I went to Calcutta to stay for several months. I was afraid of Calcutta and it had the reputation of a city dreadful at night. I arrived in the evening and as soon I booked into a hotel I immediately always went out . . .
>
> I somehow had always felt—it was an idea that I found in Nietzsche—that suffering does not exceed human capacity . . . and that is something I verified in a very personal experience with my mother's dying. It was an almost unbearable thing to watch, but she bore it with great strength and courage—and that made me believe that one does have the strength. But months later in Calcutta, the last night I was there, I took another midnight walk—I wept, really wept.

Lingis would write of death in many of his works, culminating in the big book *Deathbound Subjectivity*, the subject itself often introduced by the deaths of his mother, colleagues, students, more often presaged new friendships.

One day in Mahabalipuram, I felt death come for me. I had been bereft, in a single day, of the robust strength that once climbed the cliffs to see the cave-temples of Ajanta; within a few hours a microbe that had entered my veins through some prick too tiny to locate had drained all my strength . . . In the ten days that followed . . . I got sicker . . . Then one night I awoke from a fever to find my rib-cage rigid, my compressed lungs wheezing and choking . . . then I felt myself being lifted . . . by a small figure of a man clad only in rags. He took charge of me. He came with a cart, hoisted me on it, dragged it through the bush, located a rickshaw from someone he roused in the night, pedaled me through the jungle road, found a boat in the village by the sea, roused the owner, and laid me on it, then paddled it through the sea whose waves roared about us . . . He dragged me to the clinic in Madras. Then he left without saying a word. I would never see him again, no letter from me would ever find him.

A youth from Nepal who rowed through the storming sea with a stranger, and departed; this seemed to me a kind of nomadism radically different from the nomadism our inordinate excesses of individual value and commodity values makes possible . . . The further one goes one finds oneself only the more in oneself, the more wearied with the weight of oneself. The true nomadism is rather that which drives one, when one goes far, not to find, on each new shore on which one arrives, someone with whom one shares a language, a belief, or practical concerns, but to find someone with whom one shares nothing, the stranger, and, reduced to the solitude in which one has been mired by contracting an existence of one's own, one is delivered by the carnal arms of a stranger. If one starts with this access to the other, outside of all contracts, one will then hear the thoughts and see the perspectives and glimpse the visions of another land, without the inevitable deviation and misunderstanding and parody, the unending Western recoding. One would know *depaysment*, one would find oneself *elsewhere*.[1]

I remember that first trip for Lingis to India. I received an Aerogramme, and later a photo—writing on the back; the first of many to follow over the years.

Verily, brilliant indeed! I had written him seeking advice about my own all important dissertation back at Penn State. He unmanned my logic with a snapshot. Eventually these photo journalistic entries would become full-blown 9X12 glossy photos accompanying his annual end-of-the-year New Year greetings letter. Many would preface chapters in his books, mirroring the encounters with the strangers that sustained his jour-neys.

Tom, I write you 39 years later. I have carried those letters. They sit now before me, each one alive with dormancy. Whether it is a thought about a person or place, a shark or volcano, a simple sentence or diatribe, something would erupt with brilliance.

Introducing us to his essays in *Abuses*, Lingis said

These were letters written to friends, from places I found myself for months at a time, about encounters that moved and troubled me. . . .

The letters were almost never answered, maybe never read. Nowadays people only write letters to record requests, transactions, and detailed explanations, or to send brief greetings; when they want to make personal contact, they telephone. Conversation by telephone communicates with the tone and warmth of the human voice, but what has moved one deeply can only be shared through language when one has found the right words. Finding the right words takes time. . . .

> It is hard to share something only with words on a silent page. As the places and encounters reverberated in my heart, I found again and again they had not been said with the right words. What I wrote about them finally became too long to send to anyone. I will again find they have not been said with the right words.[2]

WE are ALL Friends in his Letters. I have always been another address. My first letter from Lingis came in 1973, written from Nice where he was raving about Deleuze who had just published his essay on Nietzsche entitled "Nomad Thought" and the urge to de-codify codes of dominant culture. Lingis certainly has followed this call to Philosophy, this impulse to cross borders; the scream to hammer them with tuning forks. He travels to places sometimes familiar, most oft strange; to peoples even farther by cultural bounds, yet near in common human grounds. Where grandeur and absurdity dwell together: in this world. Here, the letters are perhaps more direct and immediate than the published works. The letters bespeak first encounters, words written to give friends the excitement of having seen and experienced something firsthand. They are first attempts at making intelligible what nomadic Lingis perceives before the codes of conventional wisdom obscure.

A year later he wrote:

Nice, 11-22-74

chers amis—Michigan it is. The winter desolation, white serene, death, the gaping black hole before which being agonizes turns out to be made of tiny white crystals, each one different, sterile, infinite beauty. I'm afraid the hope we had that you would be shaped, by education, by grades, by judgments, by sanctions, into a Heideggerian *de l'obsérvance stricte* is going to flicker out, in that vast uncontrollable solitude. Wherever is Albion? The old Swedes with the prairie-dog eyes, knuckles color of barley, each one an Attila grimly reaping the yellow horizons? Lutherans, performing, as spiritual exercise, biological necessities in wooden back shacks while abominating the pope in Rome? Their sons in wooden benches in front of you, in rough jeans, the acrid smell of horses, hot horse muzzles, first masturbation in a stable, against the leg of the roan filly? Their daughters, nails unpainted, but hands still colored with the juice of boysenberries and black currents [sic]? Firm, pulpy breasts, big tits, not like your California nymphs, inconsistent with their heads full of theosophy. Here the purple colors of German sin, Faust and Luther, being replaced, these days, just with health, with those big tits and the Northwest air? My God, you sure as hell are out to teach them! You are going to educate yourself, wonderfully, I'll wager passing down to them all the diamonds in your course syllabuses. Plato–Johnstone–Nietzsche–Kandinsky—what is wanting? What is this indefinable lack, that something missing, that I nonetheless sniff at while reading through your class syllabuses? Sade, I suppose, or better the really sick Austrian Sacher-Masoch, Reich, Cioran, Genet, the factor of evil, sickness, the cancer on reason, the stinking effluvia. You will, coquettishly, answer that it is you yourself who will introduce that dimension. (Better, you should shrug your shoulders at the sick Rivieran who is writing to you, and look out at them, health, vigor, courage, endurance, confidence, the aching balls in those blue jeans, the big tits.) And you say they're rich yet! Old man driving bulldozers across forests, ten thousand bushels of barley or rye in the silo, three hundred black angus steers? As one who woefully has never been able to leech to any degree worth mentioning off students, and in fact have only once had one who was a genuine millionaire, himself. Yet what profession is more akin to state of mind, in that willingness to listen to, but not believe, everybody's story, bringing up the big words that flatter, that being in the street, where the men who do business with life are, that adding, at each visit, that little riff about love and eros and all that is de rigueur—what profession is more akin to that of the philosophy professor than that of the common harlot? Tant mieux si les clients sont riches . . . I am now full of projects—the top ones are to get with it on my real life-destiny, my real vocation, just now lucidly, fully recognized: to spend my life to make Levinas known. So, I am thinking about a small book, in completely accessible language, explaining what he has seen about eroticism. Then, scholarly, treatise-format, a study of temporality in Heidegger and Levinas. For Levinas, I recognize now, has a completely new idea about the internal format of present, past and future (the presence of the present, the passing-away of the past, the surprise of the future), as well as about temporalization itself, the synthetic unity that forms there, which he no longer seats in the concept of existence. This is very new I think.

To praise Lingis, to adulate, is sheer sycophancy. I plead *nolo contendere*. I am simply a flatstone, an altar upon which to worship; or to cut up dead fish. To criticize, to dispose, is sheer idiocy. Have you been there? The eros of Khajuraho, hallucinogenic nights of Borneo, Ulan Bataar, Mali, San Salvador, Cusco; the ice hotel, Pattaya transvestite bars? All of these on their New Years? This feature of his writing both attracts and frightens something in us. His descriptions have both their allure and their horror. Maybe that's why his letters are attractive: safely morphed accounts from the simulacrum. In a letter to Georges Brandes Nietzsche wrote "To my friend. George! Once you discovered me, it was no great feat to find me: the difficulty will be to lose me." If you find Lingis he will charm you. If you take him seriously, he will disarm you. Either way you could become obsessed, possessed; then again dispossessed and consumed. Does it matter? Isn't that akin to the advice Zorba the Greek gave to [his] boss: "a man needs a touch of madness, or he never dare cut the rope." Reading a letter from Lingis is a good start. Reading several letters might suck you in. As Nietzsche invited, "Either we have no dreams or our dreams are interesting. We should learn to arrange our waking life in the same way: nothing or interesting"[3] (*Gay Science* #232).

I leave you to your own readings. Here are a few of the early letters. I append scanned versions of a couple aerogrammes, mostly to highlight the precision and the economy of Lingis as typist. By 1988 he had a laptop when traveling and the scale of the letters became epic.

Shanti,
David

---

[1] Alphonso Lingis, "Being Elsewhere," in *Falling in Love With Wisdom: American Philosophers Talk about Their Calling*, eds. David D. Karnos and Robert G. Shoemaker (New York: Oxford University Press, 1993).

[2] Alphonso Lingis, *Abuses* (Berkeley: University of California Press, 1994), vii.

[3] Friedrich Nietzsche, *The Gay Science*, trans. Walter Kaufmann (New York: Vintage, 1974), 212.

Letters :: Nice, Bangladesh

I have something now to send people like you, Dave, people rumina
jubilantly over the memory of their birth--your birthday Mar 20?--
is Cioran's latest: De l'inuenvenit l'inconvenient d'être né. And it
really is about just that, not a trace of irony in the title, no last
chapter letting shine a few starbeams in the abomination of the desolation. Three hundred morose pages of considering that that chemical
accident, one's birth, was in fact the first catastrophe; ruminations
of a solitary witness without goals and purposes, watching the last
generation of humanity in its absurd works before the irreversible
cosmic night descends upon its grunts and its shrieds. Absolutely
the most nihilist book ever conceived and executed in the whole of
human history--and that includes the Buddha.
It has disturbed me most deeply. On the one side, by all in me that
is inclined to deeply agree. On the other side, by the incitation
now to think long and hard about birth, and before-birth, that void
of me--as assiduously as, these last three years, my studies around
Blandhot and Heidegger about death.
Thought for our practical lives: to reread all of Nietzsche's horril
diatribe against Wagner, in order to dig out the germ of truth in all
that: the xx vivisection of the actor. For every involvement in the
"pedagogy" of teaching people can only become that; all those years
I spent in dividing between the "full devotion to teaching these
persons" and the pursuit of my own manuscripts: there are no sages,
no gurus, no nondirective therapists; there are only actors.
Impostors. From now on: integrity, I shall henceforth only read
manuscripts in classrooms. So I trade this new year's resolution to
you.
Springtime of your life: I hope this "job hunting" becomes in fact
vocation-finding, destiny-fixing. Heideggerian wish. The Klossowsk
ian one would be: I hope it becomes not another role, butanother
mask, but another life into which you will be reborn (forgetting all
the preuterine existence up to now, feeling all the pain) with only
the certitude of having to kill it as inexorably as the cobra even
Ananda must tear off its own skin. (our world)
Remembering Nietzsche: "Que signifie aujourd'hui pour nous une
existence philosophique? N'est-ce pas presque un moyen de tirer son
épingle du jeu? Une sorte d'évasion? Et pour celui qui vit de la
sorte à l'écart et en toute simplicité, il est vraisemblable qu'il a
indiqué le meilleur chemin à suivre pour sa propre connaissance? Ne
lui faudrait-il pas avoir expérimenté cent manières différentes de
vivre pour s'autoriser à parler de la valeur de la vie? Bref,
nous pensons qu'il faut avoir vécu de façon totalement "antiphiloso-
phique", selon les notions reçues jusqu'alors, et surtout pas en xa
tant que farouche vertueux--pour juger des grands problèmes à
partir d'expériences vécues. L'homme des expériences les plus
vastes, qui les condense en des conclusions générales: ne faudrait-
il pas qu'il fût l'homme le plus puissant?--"
I shall now interrupt this letter to eat some turkey shank stewed
in orange juice, à la Shiraz.
"A former premier and foreign minister, Yem Sambo, entertains some
friends on a languid afternoon at a farewell party meal at his home.
He is going to Bangkok the next day, he explains, on a plane the
United States is using to evacuate its official personnel, foreigner
in its employ known as TCN (third-country nationals) and diplomats.
A former Cambodian premier does not seem to fit any of these categories but a member of his household explains that he has become the
honorary consul here for Haiti." Sic, the NYT wires.
We should be reading Hegel, we are for once in a spasm of history.
How can one decide how one is going to distribute the time of a
morning without being haunted by exploding planes of orphans, heros
flying single planes on dictator's palaces, a destiny of a people
being violently restructured, in poison gases, napalm, epileptic
hatreds and much, much blood.
In a week or two I shall begin to write a text on the time of a
destiny, that trajectory that arises in the cosmic chemical accident

Itinerant Philosophy

Of course I know too that it's more fun to just climb into a rickshaw, you not knowing a word of Bangla, lick your finger, test the wind, shrug your shoulders, point, giggle, and be off; eventually you will find a pad. One always does. But if when you get to Chittagong it's the middle of the night or you've got the running clap, I could recommend, Dave, the Shaikat. Because of the mirrors. Because of the narcissism of the sparrows. They just look to me like English sparrows, the ones we have back in Amerika and I suppose they tagged along somehow on the ship that brought Colonel Cox and Brigadier Billious to Bengal back in the days of the nabobs. Don't ask me how they got so narcissistic. But the Shaikat is full of them, due to the mirrors, there's one in every room.

And the thoughtfulness of the staff. Just about an hour ago ther was a godaweful screaming down the hall like a stuck pig. I went down to have a look. A couple of middle aged Chermans, with bloated white faces that looked like if you stuck a pin in them the pus would squirt out and dribble down their sweat soaked polyester wrappings; an official from some branch of the UN here to collect statistics, probab' or a representative of a pharmaceutical firm from Munich. The Frau was trembling in Auschwitzlich terror and der Mann was heroically jabbing the steel tip of his umbrella in a hole in the plaster. A rat! die Frau managed to get out. A rat! Oh, the manager said soothing and courteous, his sweet smile simmering over his rows of even gleaming teeth. He live there.

Life is brief, Dave. Why piddle around and why not just move over to where the fun is? All moral philosophy comes down to that. As I haven't been to Yemen or Mongolia or Albania I can't really say that the folk have more fun in Chittagong than anywhere, but certainly they have more fun than in most places. Be sensible, ask yourself what is the point of killing more time looking into Michigan City and then Detroit?

I wouldn't be the thinking man, the educator, the researcher I am, Dave, if I didn't ask myself, self, what is the secret of all the fun they have here in Chittagong?

So far what I've come up with is: loquacity. I never saw such a loquacious bunch. About 5AM the black of the night begins to pale and the first crow begins to mutter, and then they start. They seem to talk almost continually, every one of them. When you are talking to them they keep on talking, and then when it is their turn they shout. The tongue is the sole powerfully, even titanically built muscle in their otherwise emaciated bodies (according to the UN statistics Bangla Desh is, if one except the exceptional plight of Kampuchea, the absolute bottom in the destitution sweepstakes; the average Bangladeshi disposes of $90 worth of goods per annum, and 80% of the children are in a state of acute malnutrition).. Their tongues are like those of cobras; they get in two or three times as many words in a breath as the most longwinded whiteman. I had a little contest yesterday with the waiter and found that he could say "Brahmaputra muhlay" before I finished with "fish." What the hell are they talking about? I have no idea, I don't know the language. But since you might as well say that nothing is going on in this country there is nothing really new, thre not being anything in the way of progress, industry, publicity, , and since all these illiterates are not really exchanging views about Keynsian economics, fornication in Hollywood or Husserl's transcendental idealism, I can only assume that most of it is bullshit.And a life devoted primarily to the formulation of bullshit at high velocities is, any sage philosopher will affirm, fun.

I see that over again each time I step out of the Shaikat. I, the orangutang. (The poster at the embassy in Bangkok said "Visit Bangla Desh Before Tourists Come" That is, apparently the only come-on they could think up. No realy hurry, probably I thought at the time.) I, the orangutang step out of the front door of the Shaikat. There is a huzzah in the street, rickshaws stop in their tracks, collide, the great gray oxen suddenly rear on their haunches like kangaroos. Tender young ones scream and flee into the skirts of their fathers. Teen aged hooligans dare

Karnos: Personal Correspondences

Of course I know too that it's more fun to just climb into a rickshaw, you not knowing a word of Bangla, lick your finger, test the wind, shrug your shoulders, point, giggle, and be off; eventually you will find a pad. One always does. But if when you get to Chittagong it's the middle of the night or you've got the running clap, I could recommend, Dave, the Shaikat. Because of the mirrors. Because of the narcissism of the sparrows. They just look to me like English sparrows, the ones we have back in Amerika and I suppose they tagged along somehow on the ship that brought Colonel Cox and Brigadier Billious to Bengal back in the days of the nabobs. Don't ask me how they got so narcissistic. But the Shaikat is full of them, due to the mirrors, there's one in every room.
And the thoughtfulness of the staff. Just about an hour ago ther was a godaweful screaming down the hall like a stuck pig. I went down to have a look. A couple of middle aged Chermans, with bloated white faces that looked like if you stuck a pin in them the pus would squirt out and dribble down their sweat soaked polyester wrappings; an official from some branch of the UN here to collect statistics, probab' or a representative of a pharmaceutical firm from Munich. The Frau was trembling in Auschwitzlich terror and der Mann was heroically jabbing the steel tip of his umbrella in a hole in the plaster. A rat! die Frau managed to get out. A rat! Oh, the manager said soothing and courteous, his sweet smile simmering over his rows of even gleaming teeth. He live there.
Life is brief, Dave. Why piddle around and why not just move over to where the fun is? All moral philosophy comes down to that. As I haven't been to Yemen or Mongolia or Albania I can't really say that the folk have more fun in Chittagong than anywhere, but certainly they have more fun than in most places. Be sensible, ask yourself what is the point of killing more time looking into Michigan City and then Detroit?
I wouldn't be the thinking man, the educator, the researcher I am, Dave, if I didn't ask myself, self, what is the secret of all the fun they have here in Chittagong?
So far what I've come up with is: loquacity. I never saw such a loquacious bunch. About 5AM the black of the night begins to pale and the first crow begins to mutter, and then they start. They seem to talk almost continually, every one of them. When you are talking to them they keep on talking, and when it is their turn they shout. The tongue is the sole powerfully, even titanically built muscle in their otherwise emaciated bodies (according to the UN statistics Bangla Desh is, if one except the exceptional plight of Kampuchea, the absolute bottom in the destitution sweepstakes; the average Bangladeshi disposes of $90 worth of goods per annum, and 80% of the children are in a state of acute malnutrition).. Their tongues are like those of cobras; they get in two or three times as many words in a breath as the most longwinded whiteman. I had a little contest yesterday with the waiter and found that he could say "Brahmaputra muhlay" before I finished with "fish." What the hell are they talking about? I have no idea, I don't know the language. But since you might as well say that nothing is going on in this country there is nothing really new, thre not being anything in the way of progress, industry, publicity, , and since all these illiterates are not really radddong exchanging views about Keynsian economics, fornication in Hollywood or Husserl's transcendental idealism, I can only assume that most of it is bullshit.And a life devoted primarily to the formulation of bullshit at high velocities is, any sage philosopher will affirm, fun.
I see that over again each time I step out of the Shaikat. I, the orangutang. (The poster at the embassy in Bangkok said "Visit Bangla Desh Before Tourists Come" That is, apparently the only come-on they could think up. No realy hurry, probably I thought of at the time.) I, the orangutang step out of the front door of the Shaikat. There is a huzzah in the street, rickshaws stop in their tracks, collide, the great gray oxen suddenly rear on their haunches like kangaroos. Tender young ones scream and flee into the skirts of their fathers. Teen aged hooligans dare

Itinerant Philosophy

one another to rush up and jeer at me. Everybody waits holding his breath to see what the orangutang will do. I reach in my shirt pocket and put on my sunglasses. Thirty or forty voices are immediately raised shouting two or three hundred phonemes before ~~the utmost~~ another breath is needed. Great hilarity breaks out in the street, the bullshit, the jokes, scattering, tickling the gut into spasms, the sun flashing like prairie fire on all those big toothy grinning mouths.
I've tried, though. To keep a low profile, stiff upper lip, it's not me you see all decked out in moiré silk leggings with a sequinned codpiece and an ascot from Pierr Cardin. I bought everything I wear right here in Chittagong. This morning a young man strolled in front of me stark naked, his dingdong flapping on his thighs, and yet it was me they were all looking at so abashed.
The men, of course. Bangla Desh is a Muslim country. Women are not allowed on the streets, like Jews. If they really have to go out, say to the doctor, they cover themselves with black. Garbo should come here, instead of trying to hack it in New York. Oh well out of sight out of mind I said. Time to get over the Bangkok clap. Except that now it turns out that the clap is over but I still pee blood every fifteen minutes. I go to the doctor practically every day since I can afford it. He charges me 20 takas—about $1.15—for a consultation. Today's theory was biharzia. I told him I have been scrupulous about not wading in fresh water streams. But apparently turning on the tap and brushing your teeth amounts to the same watersnailing thing in these latitudes.
You, though? You don't have to tell me a thing. I know all about you, every detail. About the new idea you put on the table at the Merleau-Ponty circle. About how your book keeps getting bogged down in your fornication. About the dopey coed in the third row you had to give an A to last term. About the new brank of musk you have switched to. About how the football coach sucks you off two or three times a week, and how you shepherd his first string through at the end of the term. And you call yourself an atheist.

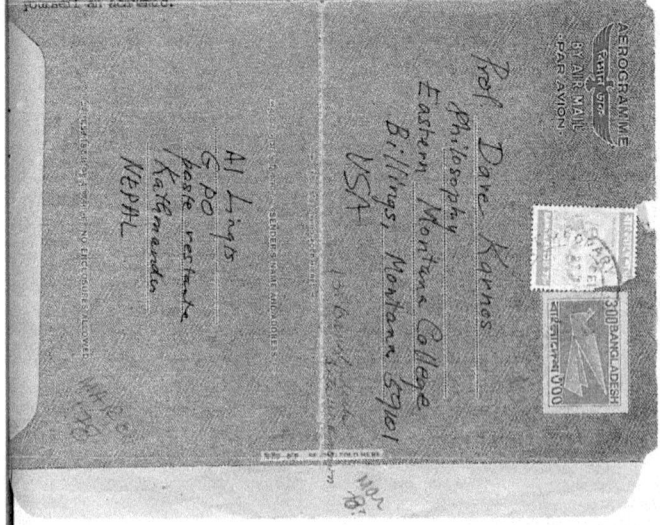

Letters :: Bogota

from: Bogota, 3/4/94

Just arrived tonight here in Columbia and turned on the tube as I unpacked and heard the Generalissimo who is running in the elections declare that four years ago, when the Liberals took over, there was terrorism and subversion in only half of the country; now it has spread to every district and province! And what a wonderful Supreme court this country has! The very day I arrived they declared any kind of criminal prosecution—and even rehabilitation programs—for the personal possession and use of cocaine, heroine, hashish, marijuana, etc. to be against the Constitution!

Here is what I wrote this last day on Te Pito O Te Henua. But oh! it's long, what I wrote. When I get a thick letter I think it's going to be tedious and a chore and some kind of requirement to answer. So do believe I am quite sincere dear Dave in saying please do not sacrifice a moment of satori, idle frolicking, cunt or ass fucking under the feeling you should read this! At the first hint of tedium throw it aside. I am only sending it to you just in case it may give you pleasure.

Te Pito O Te Henua, the Naval of the World, is the most isolated island there is, 3600 kilometers from the South American coast, 2000 kilometers from the nearest inhabited island, tiny Pitcairn where the mutineers from the Bounty settled with their Tahitian women. A pebble in the vast Pacific, it is 14.5 miles long and 7.8 at its widest point. the result of three major volcanic rises from the ocean floor (3 million, 1 million, and 600,000 years ago) and filled in by secondary volcanic cones, it is low and entirely grass covered. Long ago covered with tropical forest, it has long been treeless, and today only a few planted eucalyptus groves stand here and there to flutter the trade winds that constantly blow eastward. From the top of any of its rises, one sees the ocean all around and the curvature of the earth. Above the vastness of the sky is still more limitless. The island is a crust of volcanic cinder against which the ocean beats and sprays. There are no bays, no rivers, and no coral reefs about the island. Three volcanic craters contain lakes of rain water. Most of the surface is strewn with black chunks of jagged lava. Here and there are expanses of built-up topsoil, reasonably fertile and reasonably free of chunks of broken lava. The entire population of the island have been settled in the one village Hanga Roa. In this season, the rains are beginning with intermittent rain and drizzle and so the island is green. Tourists come—only some 4000 a year—in the dry season and for the "Easter Island Week" when they put on a "native" show. On my plane there was the inevitable group of Japanese tourists I occasionally saw in the days that followed seated in their bus with their Japanese guide, and a few stragglers as solitary as I; when we happened to arrive at the same site, the one turned away to contemplate the horizon until the other left. I stayed in a room in the house of a very old couple who spoke hardly any Spanish.

A living organism, out of the energies it assimilates from its environment, generates forces in excess of what it needs to adjust to its environment and compensate for the intermittent and superficial lacks that evaporation and fuel consumption produce in its dense and self-maintaining plenum. The discharge of these superabundant forces are felt in excremental impulses—in passions. But the environment itself is full of free and nonteleological energies—trade winds and storms, the oceans streaming over three-quarters of the planet (since the earth is porous and all the oceans interconnect, said Borges, each human has bathed in the sacred waters of the Ganges), the continental plates that float and creak and grind together, the cordilleras of the deep that explode in volcanic eruptions, and miles-deep glaciers piled up on Antarctica that flow into the sea and break off in bobbling ice mountains. How can the passions of penguins, of albatrosses, of jaguars, and of humans not lift the eyes beyond the nests and the lairs and the horizons? How can these passions not sink into volcanic rock and the oceanic deserts?

When one is there one has the impression one will stay indefinitely. The harmony of low volcanic cones and gentle grass cover under balmy skies opens about one like a benevolence. Along all the edges the island drops in sharp lava shards whipped by the ocean; beyond there is the featureless ocean and skies. There are a thousand of the giant statues, set on low stone altars on the edge of the sea facing inward, and some 15,000 other archeological sites—remains of dwellings, petroglyphs, caves.

But it is nothing like visiting a vast open-air museum, inspecting the details and decoding the significance of a thousand works of art. All the giant statues were hurled from their altars since the Christians arrived. All the smaller statues and carvings were removed by tourists and collectors; the tiny museum has only copies. Thor Heyerdahl's account of his plunder is in <u>Aku-Aku</u>, the single most sickening book I have ever read. (Worse still than the woman missionary who told me in Irian Jaya she broke into a Papuan sanctuary an danced on the altar.) Only in four sites have the statues, mostly broken, been re-erected in recent times. The statues, called <u>Moai</u>, erected over a fourteen-hundred-year period, were remarkably uniform, all very stylized busts of legendary ancestors. Out of a thousand, but three are vaguely female. Mostly one walks, since the grassy harmony of the island is so hypnotizing, and at a site one rests and enters a kind of empty reverie over the crumbled altar and the broken statue fallen face forward over the rubble. When one comes upon one of the four restored sites, there are five or seven statues on them, cemented back together if possible, very worn by the wind and the elements and the centuries. The head is as big as the chest, and there are no feet; the hands are minuscule, long fingers traced in relief over the abdomen. The head, very flat, is really just a face, turned slightly back, with strong square jaw, thin tight lips, but with huge empty eyes and strong nose with wide-open nostrils carved in a spiral. The eyes are not, like the eyes of the Buddha, turned downward compassionately on the people below. They look inward to the island, but the ocean is already visible on the other side of the low grassy width of the island. The depersonalized faces of the legendary chiefs who 1500 years ago sailed 4000 kilometers to land on that edge of crust. Stern, heretic, rigid, uniform, they certainly impose a severe order on the inhabitants, and anthropologists say early Polynesian society was very structured. But surely, in their enormity—one is estimated to weigh 300 tons— and in their eyes fixed expressionless and unbenevolent upon remoteness beyond the horizon, they did not serve to impose that structured order on the Polynesian fishermen who lived there, but demanded that order be structured for sacrifice for them. To the wanderer among them today, this stern millennial look ordering one to remote and empty distances rules one's every, increasingly aimless, step. Huge empty eyes fixed at horizons beyond this island and no doubt beyond any visible horizon. With their jaws designed by geometry, their thin tight lips, the only animation on these faces is their strong splayed nostrils, pulling in the forces of the winds.

The "mystery" of this island kept up by anthropologists seeking grants, travel writers, and tourist brochures was created by the Westerners who came upon the island, saw the statues and saw the islanders, and concluded the present-day islanders could not have created the statues; they were the work of a lost civilization colonized from the Inca of Peru, Egypt, Greeks, the lost continent of Mu, or Outer Space. Inevitably, two missionaries came to label the people cannibals. In reality linguistic studies have shown kinship of their language with that of the Marquesas, 4000 km to the east, and carbon-dating has established settlement of the island around 500 AD. Almost at once they erected giant statues; one gigantic one has been recently set upright on its altar has been dated at 690 AD. They were carved and completely polished at the quarry of the Ranu Raraku volcano then transported across the island and the eyes then carved when they were erected on their altars. How they were transported remains unexplained; the island had neither trees nor vines that could serve as cords. Recent experiments with sledges or fulcrums only proved the statues would have been ground down by the rubble on the way. There were no pack animals—indeed no mammals at all on the island—and there were no wheels invented. It is possible that they were actually carried on the back of hundreds of assembled people, then somehow set upright. The red top-knots were all quarried inside the Puna Pau volcano, then somehow rolled out and finally somehow hoisted up on the statue; many weigh 15 tons. The method used to fit together the jigsaw of separately carved stones remains as perplexing as that of the walls of Qosop. They clearly had very advanced navigational science, navigating by the stars and knowledge of sea currents and observation of birds, and must have gone on to the South American continent, since their staple food, the sweet potato, has never been found growing wild anywhere but there. But their stonework, despite Heyerdahl, could not have come from the Inca, since their culture completely lacks all distinguishing South American cultural features such as pottery, weaving, or metallurgy. They wore no clothing and instead completely covered their bodies with tattoos. They lived on the edge of the sea and fished and cultivated gardens of sweet potato, taro, and bananas. They are thought to have maintained a population of 15,000. They alone, of all the peoples of the Pacific, invented writing, rongo-rongo, partly phonetic and partly ideographic, on wood tablets. Each year these tablets were read by the chief to the whole people lasting several days in every inhabited spot of the island, and the tablets regularly copied before they showed decay. This writing, and the history, cosmology, and science it contains was lost when missionaries destroyed all but 24 pieces which had been taken out of the island by plunderers and when the chief, the sages, and all able-bodied men were rounded up by Peruvian slave-traders in 1862 to die in the guana mines.

The volcano Ranu Raraku rises out of flat landscape near the edge of the sea. The crater walls are very steep, from the top one sees the azure sky reflected on the lake within and the blue ocean beyond. All but three of the thousand giant statues of the

Itinerant Philosophy

island were quarried out of the distinctive yellowish basalt of the crater wall. Starting with the face, then the abdomen was carved and polished, working with stones of a harder basalt, until it was attached only by the rib of the spine. Recent experiments have shown it would take at least a year for a team of men to carve a small-size statue. When it was finished—save for the eyes—it was released and slid down the mountain and set upright. those that were carved inside the crater had to be moved out of it through a passage that was cut in one side of the crater. Today there are 394 statues at all stages of completion. Perhaps 75 lie fully completed at the base of the volcano; these have been covered up to the neck by the erosion and landfill from the mountain of the last 200 years. A half-dozen lie face down on the way to their final locations. Heyerdahl dug around them to expose them; they have since been covered back up to preserve the. In Cairo, in the Museum, I saw all the mummies were torn out of their tombs, stripped of their flowers and gods, and laid out in plain wood cases under glass with their faces exposed; on the walls an American scientist had put his x-ray photos of their skeletons and the urn containing the entrails of Queen Hapshetshut was split open and brightly illuminated. Ranu Rarakau is a quarry of works in progress. Should we now dig out these statues and erect them on the rebuilt altars? Philosophy too is a work in progress, cut short each time by death. Should we complete the 10th Symphony of Mahler, the working notes for Merleau-Ponty's <u>The Visible and the Invisible</u>? I spent two full afternoons completely alone among them, save for a hawk soaring above. Waiting for my death.

After living and developing their grandiose civilization for 1400 years on the Naval of the World unknown to the world, God, or themselves, the islanders were discovered by Dutch captain Jacob Roggeveen in 1722. Captain Roggeveen named the island Easter Island, shot dead thirteen and wounded many more of the inhabitants who welcomed him, and left the next day stocked up with foodstuffs. In 1770 Captain don Felipe Gonzalez arrived, landed two priests and a battalion of soldiers who advanced in procession to the center of the island, named it Isla de San Carlos, forced some natives to sign in their rongo-rongo script a Spanish document addressed to King Carlos III of Spain asking to be annexed by Spain, and left the same day. In 1774 Captain Cook arrived for a day, sent his men to search the whole island, found only 100 men and no women or children, forced the men to load up baskets of their potatoes for the scurvy-infected ship, and left. Upon opening the baskets the sailors found the people had filled them with stones, with only a covering of potatoes. In 1786 the French warship under le Comte de la Pérouse stopped on the island, and stayed 11 hours; the cove where he landed is honored today with his name. An unrecorded number of pirates, whalers, and sealers also came on the island; one recorded one was that of the USA sealer The Nancy, whose captain set out to capture the natives for slavery on his Juan Fernandez island base. He was only able to capture 12 men and 10 women. After three days at sea, he untied them; they all leapt overboard and drowned. He returned to the island to round up more. A whaler the Pindos rounded up women to take with them; they were finally shot and thrown into the sea on a drunken night. syphilis and leprosy ravaged the island. In 1862 an Armada of seven Peruvian ships commanded by Captain Aguirre lured out the people by spreading piles of cloth and foods on the beach; he was able to capture a thousand men, shooting at those who fled by land or sea, and took the captured into slavery to the guana mines of Peru. 18 more ships came in the following year. The French administrators of Tahiti and the English protested; the Peruvian authorities agreed to repatriate the slaves. Only 100 were still alive; of these 85 died on the return voyage, and the fifteen who landed were infected with smallpox which decimated the island. A Catholic missionary was brought in, the people converted, the remaining statues overthrown, the rongo-rongo tablets burnt, and the family collections of heirlooms, statues, and wood carvings, said not to be the work of demons, were destroyed. The missionary also brought in tuberculosis. In 1872 French writer Pierre Loti arrived on a warship, they hurled one of the remaining statues down to break off the head which they loaded on the ship; it is now in the Musée Trocadero in Paris. In 188 Chile annexed the island, rounded up the now total population of 111 in a corral at Honga Roa, and allotted the rest of the island to sheep ranchers. Few Chileans were interested; it was the British who bought all the concessions and turned the island over to 70,000 sheep who denuded the island of its shrubbery and at the grass to the roots. Too far for economic transportation, they were eliminated in recent years and replaced by horses and cattle. In 1934 French anthropologist Alfred Métraux did the first cultural exploration of the island; the Chilean government was persuaded of its tourist possibilities and in 1935 made most of it a National Park. In 1986, after the explosion of the Challenger, the US NASA program built an airstrip for recuperation of satellite descents into the Pacific.

Somewhere half-way through grade school I brought up a linguistic problem to the teacher. She (and the textbook) called the Roam civilization a great civilization. Its greatest period was the period when its military domination was over the greatest number of lands and peoples. When its empire shrunk, it was said to be in decline. This vocabulary continued to be used in history class after history class throughout my schooling, and in museum after museum I visited since. The great religions are the world religions. Civilization is intrinsically tied up with military and economic expansionism. The euphemism is competition—without competition there is no artistic, literary, or religious advance. (Without grades, prizes, honors, there is no philosophical achievement.) My first trip was t Florence, where I was beset by the evidence that all its artistic, literary, and musical achievements coincided with its richest and most rapacious century; as soon as that was over, it could only sigh on in mannerism. Today it is rich through tourism, but without political expansionism its artistic and literary culture is comparable to that of Oklahoma City. Now that France has lost its empire, there is no more philosophy there. Culture is the glory of a civilization—and that glory is the glint of advancing swards and missiles. The frantic theories of Thor Heyerdahl and the others striving to prove that the sculpture and the walls on Te Pito O Te Henua were imported from the Inca, from Egypt, Greece, India, or China are based on the conviction that an isolated culture always declines.

I crisscrossed Te Pito O Te Henua many times, over this crust of volcanic cinders covered with grass, ending up inevitably at the emptiness of the featureless sea and the curvature of the earth under the unending flow of wind and sky. The small flowers one sees in the grass one sees everywhere. There are no coral reefs swarming with fish to attract sea birds and sea mammals. The few sparrows and small hawks one sees are recent imports. No rodents or lizards scurry through the chunks of lava. There are no cliff formations like fortresses; only the harmonious low cones of volcanoes extinct a million years ago. The 15,000 people who lived here for 1400 years did not divide up into rival clans; the ruler continued the hereditary line unbroken from the founder Hotu Matu's and the thousand giant statues that surround the rim of the island show only a gradual stylization over a thousand years. The passion that built this civilization was not driven by competition. It was passion—a nowise conservative, economic, or rational but an excessive drive to erect 300-ton statues of completely depersonalized faces with eyes looking out into the featureless emptiness. This passion worked with volcanoes and the wind and the ocean and the sky.

Orongo is an extinct volcano; its crater lake is a perfect circle a mile wide. On one side of the crater the land continues in a cliff a thousand feet over the sea. Where the cliff meets the volcanic crater is the sacred precinct of Mata Ngarau. The boulders are covered with petroglyhs—1785 have been counted. On the very edge of the cliff there are 47 dwellings. From above they form clusters of round grass-covered circles. The walls of these circular dwellings are made of uncemented sheets of slate laid flat and corbelled. The entrances are at ground level, just two feet high and so narrow one has to lift one side of one's torso to crawl inside. Inside they are covered with paintings. They are the residence of the priests of the birds. Below in the sea there are two islands, one a stalagmite rising abruptly out of the sea, the second a stone outcropping. They are the nesting places of the migratory terns, the manu-tara. Each year when the manu-tara returned, the tangata-manu, the birdmen chosen in dreams by the priests at Mata Ngarau were paramount throughout the island, not so much ruling as descending upon its settlements in orgiastic raids.

The bird culture is a late dominance of an aboriginal stream of this civilization. The founding king Hotu Matu'a who had set sail with the original colonizers in the fifth century was surely led to this minuscule island by birds. The colonists had brought with them poultry, which remained their only domestic animal. They had also brought with them their Marquesas deities, which were gradually supplanted by Makemake, the god of the bird culture. But for 1400 years the culture was structured, heratic, under hereditary rulers. It was in the 17th century, when the island became prey to plunderers from the outside, the millennial-old temples overturned, the people hiding in closed volcanic caves at the first sight of any foreign ship on the horizon, that this period called "anarchy" by Western writers came about. The ancient heritary kings (ultimately all to die in slavery in Peru) were replaced by men whose prowess naked in the raging sea marked them to be temporary sovereigns. But their sovereignty was not an administration of a structured society that no longer existed, it was a pure celebration of a power that was proud, orgiastic, and violent. Not a panicky totalitarian culture bent on preserving its sedentary economy from the depredations of yet more rapacious agents of the mercantile societies of the Dutch, English, French, Russians, and Peruvians, but, in the ruins, the liberation of a totally different kind of culture. Culture of force, daring, pride, violence, and eroticism. Culture of birds.——

Letters :: China, Uzbekhistan

Got some news of you dear David from Walt and Dorothea at the SPEP meeting--that you have purchased land and will build on it! How wonderful. They also told me how much they loved your partner. You will have ever more energetic and creative hours. I think of your beloved students happy to come help, and your native American friends coming in greater numbers for extended visits.

A friend came up with the idea that now is the time to extend NATO and the European economic union to all countries and seriously build world government. I was very struck with this idea; it is actually doable. But meantime the grotesque image of the richest country in the world pounding the poorest with missiles costing two million each.

I am leaving tomorrow for China--and on United Airlines; one does have to seek out excitement. The meeting itself is wonderfully ridiculous: Beijing University is hosting the "First" International Phenomenological Conference, on the occasion of the centenary of Husserl's *Logical Investigations*, and we invitees are limited to speak but 20 minutes. Imagine the absurdity of flying to the other side of the planet to talk 20 minutes and flying back. But of course 20 minutes is all anyone could endure listening to raps on that book; indeed the speakers themselves could not endure the boredom of talking more than 20 minutes about it.

Global warming has brought us summer weather till now; today feels like August. I have acquired a pair of poison arrow frogs which, of course, I put in the bedroom next to the bed, and a sting ray. And for the garden a pair of ruffed grouse and a pair of Edward's pheasants. These are endemic to Vietnam only, and were discovered by brit Reginald Edward, since the Vietnamese were too stupid to have noticed them. They are extinct in Vietnam, wiped out by Agent Orange, and survive only in captivity. So I am delighted to offer my little garden as a sanctuary for this supremely endangered species.

In Uzbekistan I finished a book, rather of the genre of *Abuses*; I am calling it *Trust*. I do so like that word, and also the experience.

Cordial wishes for happy days on the range!

Love
Al

How could I not be thinking of you dear Dave, peering around at the tracks left by the Xiongnu, Kushans, Huns, Sogdians, Ghaznavids, Karakhanids, Khorezmshahs, Mongols led by our friend Chinggis Khan, The Golden Horde of Batu and Ord, the Middle Horde of Chaghatai, the Third Horde of Ogedai Khan and of course Kublai Khan, and then Timur (not Tamerlane), the Oyrats and the Zhungarians--all galloping down from your sister land of Mongolia to do what they did best: terrorize, loot, pillage, plunder, rape! What times they had! What, after all, would you do, were you a nomad with nothing to do all day but keep an eye on your horses and sheep and goats getting fat over grasslands stretching as far as eye can see, and in fact stretching from China to Hungary, and along came a Khan out of Mongolia who said hey man leave us go terrorize Beijing, loot Delhi, Pillage Bagdad, plunger Damascus, rape Constantinope--could you, dear Dave, resist, say: Oh shoot boys I think I'll hang around with these here sheep and goats, maybe next summer?
And you dear Dave here's hoping you are having great times over in sister Montana, may it be the best of all summers!

It has been a wandering summer for me, I now see in the spirit of the great Central Asian nomads. Started in Athens for a first look at the Parthenon, then to Jerusalem for a look at the doings of War Criminal Ariel Sharon, then to the Red Sea to dive and to see my first manta ray. The book says they attain a wingspan of 22 feet and can weigh 7 tons! The mum gives birth to a single pup, who is 1 meter long at birth and 10 kilos. The one we saw was maybe 6-7 foot wingspan so must have been a kid. Of course to keep one in the house, I will have to extend my basement tank in tunnels under the adjacent property lots. Project for the fall.

Then to Cairo to spend an hour alone in the second biggest pyramid, just opened to, but not yet known to, the public. And to spend a night mindfuckedly ecstatic watching the dervishes whirl. Then to Petra in Jordan, where the Nabateans filed through a crevice in the continental plate and carved the rock walls with hundreds of facades without rooms behind, making the mountain itself into a gigantic palace.

Then to Turkey, and to Sanliurfa and to the cave there where, on March 19, 2100 BC, Abraham was born. I knelt in the cave and washed my faces with the sacred spring that flows from there, and then strolled about the ponds full of carp which Abraham as a kid sprang into life by whooshing a stick in the water, the whole place arcaded in white with a mosque of the most exquisite classical taste. But I kept thinking: Hey 2100 BfuckinC: that's a hell of a *l o n g* time ago! How do we know that the kid that was born in this cave is the right Abraham--the one who huffed and fucked and puffed out Jewry? How do we know it's not that *other* Abraham--the one that also got born in a cave, also tended his father's flocks of sheep and fucked his father's goats, then decided it would be more

Karnos: Personal Correspondences

glamorous to be an artist, took up painting using goatblood and jism, went down to Damascus where like Van Gogh never sold a single one of his paintings but indulged in the bohemian life of artists and died of acute alcoholism--*that* Abraham?

And for the last month in Uzbekistan, wallowing in the awesome gorgeousness of the stupendous mosques, medressas, caravanserais built in the age of Timur in Samarqand, Bukhara, and Khiva, where the Silk Road camel caravans from China joined the yak caravans coming over and down the Himalayas laden with jewels and spices from India, before heading on to Bagdad, Damascus, Cairo and Rome. The Russian Tsar finally annexed the region in 1868, while the brits were expanding their empire up from Indian into Tibet and Afghanistan. But the folk here have not forgotten those glory days! The way you can tell who in the street is Russki and who Uzbek is that all the Uzbeks, as soon as their teeth reach maturity, have them completely crowned in gold. A young lad would not have a chance of dating an eligible chick if he did not have all his teeth capped in gold. And a chick gets her teeth all gold capped for her engagement. Land of the golden smiles! Down the street, there is a four-foot-high vulture on a leash. I feed him kebabs.

And, in Samarqand, the tomb of Daniel, the Biblical prophet, his remains brought here by no less than Timur himself, to lie next to the lion's den, scene of Daniel's biggest triumph. His body has been growing a half inch a year, and so the sarcophagus is 18 meters long. So it is good for 1368 years--Timur was a forward looking man!

In my copy of *The Utterances of Amir Timur*, the Little Gold Book of course, we read :

> I distinguished between two types of advice one coming from lips and the other from the depth of heart. I lent a willing and favorable ear to what the lips said but it was only what I heard coming from the heart that I kept in the ears of my heart.

love
A

Letters :: Jayapura

from: Jayapura, December, 1988

Dear Zoltan--Upon returning to Bangkok from Ho Chi Minh City I had the pleasure of a day eating fish-intestines and fondling transsexuals with Karim, thinking of our buddy you, who is preparing to join us paging through images of the deep and sucking your milk from a rubber cock. It is of course you who bond us together, and then Karim went on to scout the lay of China for you and I your advance man to Jakarta. For Heideggerians we are, Daseins who exist by hurling ourselves into the future from which meaning comes, that meaning which is not form but possibility. Here is our first report...

Your old man wanted to take you from the cradle directly to Huntsville with the commendably Heideggerian but mistaken idea that the future, and meaning, lies in NASA but of course expecting to have the right direction pointed out to one by family is antediluvian, and it is Karim in rural China and I in Jakarta who have credibility.

Rural China, and not the ersatz Wall-Street-and-Hollywood that the television cameramen shoot in the immediate vicinity of their five-star hotels in Shanghai to satellite back to ABC and NBC for use in 14-second sound bites on the world they report on. They don't stray out there in rural China; they would never find their way back. Karim, the most clairvoyant of the futurist Daseins we know, was gracious enough to have sent me a report on rural China edited by Serres a full year before his departure for it. Rural China, consisting in minuscule picture-puzzle pieces of paddy, where there is not yellow-clay clod of surplus-value mud, to speculate with, not a single frog or grub or weed that are just spectacle: everything is eaten. Not a square yard spared by the hunger of the peasant; the lotus is eaten, tuberous roots roasted, leaves boiled, flowers sauteed, seeds ground and mixed into the rice-flower dough. No hedge rows left in thickets for wildlife; the paths are the tops of the walls of the paddy fields. They lead the peasant from his house to his fields and back again. Beyond that, they meet with paths of the next village. If during his lifetime he goes further than his fields, it will be to the next village to bring back a wife. There are no thoroughfares, no highways leading the peasant beyond and outside. The end of civilizing history; nomadism, migration is totally abolished; if the peasant were to wander or migrate it would be only to another village with lanes that likewise lead from the house to the fields and back again. Here civilization, the sedentary existence, is exclusive and accomplished already several thousand years ago, before the West began its provincial, brief and temporary, experiment with linear history. Here rationality is realized, in the total occupancy of all the space, in the total usage of all the resources, in every clod of clay, every weed and every frog surviving only because it has a purpose, the universal and necessary purpose of serving as alimentation. So that the peasant who exhausts his body resources today working in the fields will be able to return to the fields tomorrow, so that he will reproduce other peasants like himself to replace him at these fields. Rural China then is both the End, the goal and the terminus, of Rational History, and the termination of history in Eternity, an Eternity in repetition that was put in place before linear history began.

It is rural China that gives you the vision of the future and end of provincial Western linear history, whose linear phase is provisional and transitory. The view your old man thought to give you by taking your cradle to porch with a view onto the NASA launching pads is a myopic one; you would see only the young men with the right stuff marching like pioneers and conquerors into the space capsules, and you would see the linear trajectory of the take-off in a blast that dazzles out the light of the sun. You would not see that this line quickly curves out into a circle that orbits upon itself indefinitely.

Your old man would of course smile if he read this, this idea that rural China is the future and goal of Western linear history. "Another far-fetched fantasy of that nostalgic Lithuanian peasant Lingis," he would say, blinking myopially. As we kids understand, one really cannot expect a kid to get reliable guidance from his old man.

Anyhow it was the citizen Karim that went to rural China and the peasant Lingis that went to Jakarta to scout the future for you.

On the simpleminded argument that the future will be urban and not rural, intellectuals like your old man go to London, Paris, Rome. There they look at a few streets of old buildings recycled into restaurants and boutiques, go to a museum to look at some 15th century altarpieces and to an opera house to listen to some 18th century court music.

But it is the new cities of the third world--Mexico City, Jakarta, Calcutta, Manila, Bangkok--where urbanization has to be understood. 10% of the Thais now live in Bangkok; 12% of the Javanese in Jakarta. It is there that the total rational occupancy of the land is realized (the real estate value of the land within the Tokyo city limits is greater than that of the land of all rural Amerika).

The cities of the future are the interminable labyrinths of rural China where the clay walls of the paddies are solidified in cement cubicles and where the paths are electronic leading the citadin without leaving his computer terminal to the adjacent and equivalent computer terminal. Fed in bytes which permit him to reproduce himself with other computer-operators to replace him when he dies.

Your old man would of course smile if he read this, this idea that to become Jakarta is the future and goal of London, Paris, Rome, New York. "Another far-fetched fantasy of that Lingis from a marginalist and provincial place like Lithuania," he would say. "Every knows that if one were ever to actually go to third world cities one would get engulfed in swarming masses of lumpenproletarians as soon as one stepped out of one's hotel." Really one cannot expect a kid to get reliable guidance from his old man.

It is true that if one went to London, Paris, Rome (places where nobody can get a philosophy job these days with howevermany and howeverlaserprinted recommendation letters), one would meet only computer programmers. Whereas third world Cities are distinctive in that one is forced to recognize by the fact that one cannot help being engulfed in swarms of them that they are vast social factories that produce lumpenproletarians.

But: the third world lumpenproletarians shall inherit the earth.

And if you, dear Zoltan, are to Heideggerianly be a Dasein existing by receiving meaning from the future, it will be necessary for you to become a third world lumpenproletarian. This will have to be done by actually meeting third world lumpenproletarians and learning all the future things directly from them. It cannot be done by learning the merely negative, privative definitions of third world proletarians from the old man and his books. Happily, you have kids like Karim and me to do some preliminary scouting and advancing reporting to you.

One will never learn all their dialects, and they never know anything but the same few phrases of Pidgin. Verbal communication then has always the same content and is exhausted in the first five minutes.

In those five minutes one reaches the state the contemporary Western sciences and technologies of communication will leave us in fifty years.

For what is happening now is that all possible messages are formatted electronically in codes that can be instantly transmitted on every computer terminal, all possible secrets (of celebrities, politicians, priests) are beamed by satellite everywhere in the planet and flashed on public buildings in letters ten stories high in all the Times Squares of the World. There will be nothing further for one citadin to communicate with another when they meet; their conversation will be limited to repeating the same stock phrases "How are you? Where are you from? How do you like Jakarta?" which exhaust conversation with a third world lumpenproletarian now.

But after this five-minute conversation in esperanto English, one lingers on, to learn and to enter into the language of the future, that of third world lumpenproletarians. Not the language of humans which is only of humans, of their egos, the desiccated spoor excreted by their egos, that language of their sordid and greedy secrets now instantly projected on the walls of buildings in the Times Squares.

This language is the nocturnal voice of third world Cities. In the mucky slums of Jakarta as the sun sets the frogs begin, a din of rumbles, heavings, explosions, emanations of sultry humus where the frogs extend their proximity to one another in a sonorous environment without messages. As third world Proletarians pass one another they resonate their proximity with such rumblings, heavings, explosions, incantations. Utterances of frogs, insects, birds, mice, bats, creaking coconut trees and shifting bamboo thickets, cascading or dripping waters, winds.

Voices of the sea and of the winds, language of the resounding universe, of which the human throat and respiratory tubes are but a channel.

Another thing one will learn from third world lumpenproletarians is how to dress. Nothing arouses their contempt more readily than coming to them costumed in the fake-prolo of backpackers. No third world lumpenproletarian can relate to a whiteman from Huntsville who hasn't shaved this morning, who doesn't bathe at least three times a day, who is wearing a shirt with yesterday's sweatstains in the armpits, who is fat and balding. (Rich whitemen dress down, third world poorpeople dress up, was the way I formulated it in a maxim for the usage of practical judgment to Bob and Denise in Bangkok.) Rich whitemen from Huntsville do not present their selves to one another; they parade before one another with a body-armor of their "soul," their characters, their professions, their educations, their histories, their jobs, their achievements. It is that informed APS journalist, that Penn State football player, that intertextual deconstructionist, that department chairman they encounter. With third world lumpenproletarians it is the dark henna-dyed gleaming eyes, the sinuous islander, the mustachioed macho Salvadoran, the sassy-assed Jamaican, the Siamese slum kickboxer you encounter. In Bali, the very land of the bare-breasted women, there is everywhere posted the most stern warnings against tourist nudity, a whitewomyn who goes skinnydipping, a white male who is seen on a motorcycle without a long-sleeved shirt or in shorts is immediately arrested. That has nothing to do, in that Hindu-animist land, with any Judeo-Christian sexual hangups; it is simply that they just can't stand the sight of how ugly we are.

The lower down you go in the castes of India, the more the women are covered with jewels, diamonds on their nostrils, gold chains hanging from the septum of their noses to their ears, silver cobras around their ankles. Nothing is more difficult than to buy a t-shirt for a rickshaw puller friend, so exacting is his taste in color, fabric, cut, design; they would certainly never wear any of the beach clothing their wives sew up for the tourists. I have found from experience that the only method is to go with him to the market and restrict yourself to paying for the one he has selected.

Among whitemen their wealth in things, their education, their professions, their jobs free them. Among third world Proletarians beauty liberates. The beauty of a woman frees her from her village, will one day free her from the brothel, frees her from the man who wants to own her, frees her unwanted children, frees her from the interdictions of morality and religion and from the police. The macho splendor of a man frees him from responsibilities and judgment. Frees him from wealth, educations, professions, jobs. It is a physical, corporeal beauty, that frees one to be without rival, to be in competition with no other image than one's own...

The most important, the most inconceivably difficult, the most ecstatic-hurl-into-the-future a Dasein can find among those transsexuals-of-the-future is the staggering, electrifying plunge into a relationship with others that is one of pure lust.

All parents instinctually know they have no more implacable enemy than pure lust ("the dirty old man"); all the educational institutions that function in *loco parentis* are brainwashing centers of the disciplinary archipelago which format in a complete ethical-metaphysical-cosmological ideology designed the block out like a virus on the RAM of a youth's cerebral circuitry pure lust (cf. the recent hysteria generating "sexual harassment penal procedures") For out of lust comes all understanding. It is pointless to leaves one's cubicle and computer terminal in the space capsule being manufactured for you in Huntsville if you go with your set of educated ideas, information, skills, profession, all those plastic credit cards that reformulate all the rupiahs and dong and rials and tjats into dollars and cents. You will never see the culture of the lumpenproletarian slums of Jakarta; you will only record on your own meter sticks, balances, and stop watches the pluses and the minuses, in fact the minuses.

It is when alone, hot, sweating, unable to sleep, unable to reach anyone back home on the phone to talk with, unable to read, unable to think, you are reduced to a lustful body turning in the night, that drives you out into the night, it is then when, finding yourself in the arms and orifices of a third world lumpenproletarian, nameless, any profession or none, any age or gender, that your body, your glands, your orifices craves for, it is then that, finally, you will be in the spiritual condition finally in which it will be possible to advance with love into the language the other loves, the dress the other loves, the gestures the other loves, the human bonds the other loves, the myths and the idols the other loves. In short, to discover his or her or his/her land and history and culture.

Things of course no kid ever could hope to get through to his old man and old lady.

Letters :: Lima

from: Lima, July 1990

Hey did you catch it over there dear Walt? Lucky man you are, that you have a real ace reporter who recognized the kind of news you want to hear and can fly it to you by macaw express. Stop the presses, this is the BIG ONE. HERE IT IS MAN, FROM ON THE SPOT AND RIGHT ON THE DAY:

!!!!! THE PRISON BREAK! !!!!!!!!!!OF THE CENTURY! !!!!

Inaugurated in 1986, the Castro Castro Penitentiary was presented s the pilot maximum security prison of Latin America. Video cameras and motion detectors observed every square foot of the cells and corridors. The cells could be opened only with an electronic system similar to that installed in the latest federal penitentiary in Miami. IT was named for Miguel Castro Castro, director of the El Fronton penal island, assassinated by the Sendero Luminoso as he was leaving his home, after the great police massacre of Sendero Luminoso prisoners in 1986. The Penitentiary was laid out in panoptical architecture, about a central watch-tower. It was designed for 700 inmates. Yesterday it contained 3800, most of them guerrillas captured in the civil war raging for the past ten years in Peru.

Today, July 9, there are 48 less. Victor Polay Campos, "Camarada Rolando," head of the MRTA, the Tupac Amaru Revolutionary Movement, and 47 others, 9 of them women, of the same organization have escaped (among them the commando that had killed 16 policemen and the terrorist that had planted the bomb that blew up the Kentucky Fried Chicken right in the heart of Lima). Polay had been captured and imprisoned 17 months ago and was to have been sentenced today. He was the most important insurgent the army had captured in the ten years of the civil war.

The escape is surely the most spectacular in history.

Some two years ago, a young couple, Victor and Rosa Vargas, and their niece Sonia, rented a small half-constructed building located about a quarter-mile from the penitentiary. Vargas had a blue Dodge pickup truck, and left daily at 4:30 in the morning, loaded with construction sand from the site. Like so many structure sin this slum area, his building was half-collapsed, and Vargas often unloaded building materials, when he returned. Other men sometimes came with him and left late; the neighbors assumed they were helping him on construction after working hours. The adjacent building was a small diner, where police from the Penitentiary came to lunch. Rosa, attractive and submissive, often sat in front of the house, and parried their flirtations.

The stupefied police today discovered that below this house a tunnel of some 800 meters was dug into the core of the Penitentiary. The entrance was found under a wardrobe. From there the tunnel descended 30 feet, zigzagged around underground sewer and power conduits, descended to 50 feet under the penitentiary wall, to open last night in the toilets of the cell block where the MRTA inmates were incarcerated. since the subsoil here is gravely, the walls and ceiling of the tunnel were made of concrete.

Engineers studying the construction estimate that the materials alone had cost $200,000. They also affirm that only expert topographers could have designed the tunnel that it arrive exactly at the cell block to which it was destined. It was illuminated throughout with electricity, tapped from the penitentiary power lines themselves. It was even air conditioned, equipped with walkie-talkies, oxygen tanks and masks, emergency medical resuscitation equipment, and contained large quantities of food. Engineers believe it must have taken a year to build, and 500 cubic meters of earth had to be removed daily.

In the early morning a commando of three entered the tunnel and made their way to the cell block of the MRTA. The women were in a separate building. Polay was in the maximum security cells on the third floor adjacent to the prison command post itself. to reach the others once freed, he would have had to cross five guard posts. Only two guards were killed. The 48 inmates descended the tunnel and emerged into a waiting stolen police van, where they changed into police uniforms, and were driven to a Cessna waiting in a gorge outside Lima. It took off for a recently earthquake-devastated zone of the Upper Huallaga. Discarded film boxes showed police they had even videotaped their escape.

The government immediately ordered the most massive manhunt ever launched in the country; within hours more than 20,000 were detained. The country was put on red alert; borders were sealed. As of now no trace of the escapees. But in the heart of Lima a government bus was stopped and incinerated by a commando of the Sendero Luminoso—on Avenida Tupac Amaru. The message, as always, as left to the army and public to decipher; the Sendero Luminoso never signs or leaves explanations when it attacks.

Tupac Amaru was the Inca who led the massive rebellion against Pizarro in 1536. The Tupac Amaru Revolutionary Movement was founded in 1984 with a raid on the National Museum of Huaura that captured the sword and the flag San Martin used in proclaiming the Independence of Peru in 1821, and with an occupancy of Radio Independencia, which forced the reading of its program on the airwaves. This movement split from the Sendero Luminoso, pledging itself to strict accord with the Geneva convention with regard to sparing innocents and noncombatants, and the treatment of captives. While the Sendero Luminoso is principally based in the Upper Huallaga mountains, the Tupac Amaru's zone of action is in the cities. And its actions have been characterized by their spectacular effects. It began with several attacks of the US Embassy in 1884. It exploded a bomb within the Ministry of the Interior. Last October it captured the director of Panamerican Television, whom it liberated with orders to show on television a video prepared in which he is shown negotiating for the government the purchase of Mirage planes.

Victor Polay Campos, 39 years old, is the son of one of the founders of the now-ruling APRA party, a classmate and even, while in Europe, a roommate of President Alan Garcia. One of his sisters was a senatorial candidate of the APRA party in the recent election. It was while a student at the Sorbonne in Paris that he became disillusioned with APRA politics and returned to Peru to found the MRTA.

Drugs and Violence!

Becoming-Troglodyte

by Joff Peter Norman Bradley

This essay mines the phenomenal oeuvre of Alphonso Lingis to explicate his theory of communication. It is argued that there is such a theory and it is one intimately and inextricably linked with a philosophy of community. Cartographically and genealogically, to chart how his theory of communication has taken shape, I shall draw on a number of thinkers who have informed his thought over the years. While completing such a task presents formidable exegetical challenges, this essay claims that while Lingis indeed has a theory of communication, it is one synthesized and inflected by an eclectic reading of continental philosophers such as Bataille, Deleuze and Guattari, Levinas, Merleau-Ponty, and Nietzsche, among others.

However, this foray into the thickets of his dense and richly descriptive prose aims not to reproduce verbatim what Lingis has penned in his translations, numerous lectures, books, and monographs, because extrapolating a consistent theory is a difficult, nigh impossible task to accomplish, given, and by his own omission, Lingis's thought-experiments do not always form a consistent whole. And in another way, it is perhaps wise to resist the urge to render the fragmentary writings of Lingis into some form of pristine totality: to say terminally what he *should* have said, to say at the end *yes that is what he meant*. His writings are best understood if the reader appreciates his monographs are honed in to a particular time, place, and ethical moment. His thought-experiments are sometimes performative and material, primed for a particular muse on the nature of things. It is therefore difficult to think Lingis as writing an oeuvre of a single trajectory across time and space. His writings are specific to location, solitary perspective, and singular theme.

LEVINAS

Levinas' influence on Lingis cannot be underestimated. It is difficult not to hear Levinas' voice when one reads Lingis. Indeed, Lingis discerns in Levinas a philosophy of limits, a philosophy of the limits of language, the limits of *the said*. Lingis, following Levinas, scrutinises the idea of non-relationality to the other. The other is irreconcilable difference, beyond commonly held bonds and shared thoughts, on the thither side of *das gerede*. For Lingis, the fundamental relation of the self to the other is prior to that which is common. Heterogenic difference to alterity is pre-ontologically ethical. There is an inescapable appeal before any information is bartered or shared.

Today theories of communication induce us to depict the others about us as agencies with which we exchange information. But when we actually communicate with people about us, the exchange of information is the least part of our conversation; most of the time we utter words of welcome and camaraderie, give and receive clues and watchwords as how to behave among them and among others, gossip, talk to amuse one another. The other is evidently there, a person, for us not as an agency that issues meaningful propositions, information, but as an agency that orders us and appeals to us.[1]

Lingis investigates the intrusive horror and overwhelming proximity of the other. The relation to the other is one of exposure, vulnerability, and sensibility. Above all, the 'I' is essentially contested by the other and is irrevocably responsible. The relation is one of precarity. The proximity of the other implies the suppression of ethical distance, as one is bound to reciprocate and respond. The self is fissured. Subjectivity is constituted heteronomously as the other is *anarchical*. For Lingis, the self-legislating, autonomous subject of Western reason is undermined in such a non-relation to the other, and subjectivity is subjection to the infinite demands of the other, to an uncertain compassion.[2] As he says: "Thought is obedience; subjectivity is constituted in subjection."[3] And again, in discussing the defenestration of Gilles Deleuze, Lingis writes: "Becoming someone who stands on his or her own and speaks in his or her own name—subjectification—is then subjection and subjugation.[4]

The responsibility for another is precisely a saying prior to anything said. For Lingis, as for Levinas, language is precisely the expression of a relation prior to the transmission of ideas. Communication with things is not extraction of information or data, but of finding oneself invaded and populated. The saying as communication is exposure. Proximity and communication are not modalities of cognition *per se* as communication is irreducible to the process of transmitting messages from one ego to another. Moreover, communication exceeds the data from the signals sent from one ego to another. It is something other than the simple transmission and reception of signs. Communication is more than its contents.

At the limit of communication is the gesture towards the other. It is at the limit of communication which for Lingis gives rise to communication as an ethical event. It is in irreconcilable alterity that we locate a fundamental relationship with the other. The relation to the other *qua* other is a non-relation, the quintessence of communication. For Levinas in *Totality and Infinity*, first philosophy is an ethics.[5] As such, the concern for the other is pre-ontological; it is formed neither through rational calculation nor contract. More fundamentally still, it is the very basis of ethically heteronomous subjectivity, which is decentred through exposure and openness, through a subjection to the other. Moreover, subjectivity is constituted through a vulnerability and sensibility, and concern for the other is located precisely in this responsibility.

One is exposed, presented as vulnerable and sensitive to the other who appears as a face. It is through the face that the other addresses me silently and makes demands upon me. The face is the locus for the beginning of language. Through its silence, the face beseeches. And in terms of the proximity of the face, there is a suppression of ethical distance.

Levinas in his discussion of language makes a distinction between the sayable and the said.[6] Briefly expressed, the said is the material of language which imparts information, knowledge, and meaning by means of representation. It registers the correlation between a thing and the thought of that thing. The said brings the world into language and language into the world by eliding the difference between things and words.

On the other hand, the saying expresses a relation to the one being spoken to. It signifies a modality in the approach to the other. Language is therefore an expression of relation rather than the simple transmission of ideas. Language *qua* the saying is an expression of relation, of drawing close to the other, of proposing a proposition to the other. For Levinas, the responsibility for another is precisely a saying prior to anything said. The saying, still entwined in the said, impresses before it makes sense; it affects before it effects.

Contact is therefore the elemental relation, the groundless foundation of ethical relationship. This is vital for Lingis's communication theory as he is interested in the ways in which language make contact and touches. Heidegger interprets common knowledge as a multiplicity of statements that circulate, that are picked up and passed on from one to another. The speakers appear as simple relay points, equivalent and interchangeable with one another. Statements are enunciated and repeated because they are of what is said; anyone and everyone says them. No one speaks in his own name, no one takes responsibility for what is said. In fact, the talk does not just circulate in all directions, as interlocutors are not merely the relay-points of anonymous refrains. They are ordered. There are directions and directives in the talk. For Lingis, who sees in language something more fundamental at work, Heidegger was bound to misinterpret this as he reduces the function of the talk to that of communicating information and hence not the phenomenology of the unsayable.

Thinking as Material and Performative

Philosophy in the Lingisian mode is multi-mediated performance as it conveys a wider philosophical message. Lingis's methodology is to ruminate on the limits of the sayable. His utterances are made against a backdrop and background of images, music, and noise. For the audience there is some confusion as to what is being said, what meaning is being expressed. While it is debatable that this is always successful, Lingis is trying to express or murmur something more fundamental. The words that come from the philosopher's mouth are perhaps only part of the tapestry of meaning. The disembodied voice is posited as secondary as Lingis's mode of communication bespeaks of different ways of expression and languages, of something more elemental. There is Lingis dressed as geisha, Lingis speaking against a cacophony of Latin American music, Lingis speaking in the dark, with only torchlight to read his script. And scattered throughout his books are photographs of faces, faces from different races, cultures, across time and places. Faces which disrupt and unnerve, which interrupt his text. He is a philosopher who dares to live in a world of shadows, where nothing is certain, to play with masquerade and camouflage. He is a thinker who transports his readers away from the world of light to the dark and dingy places of the world, to culturally subterranean pockets of resistance to the banality of things.

Seemingly contrary to honouring the logos of Western metaphysics, he becomes ichthyophagan so as to speak from the cave, from the shadows, or the nether world. He becomes troglodyte, a cave dweller, in order to know other worlds, to speak of the worlds, to nestle in these worlds. Yet, how can these subterranean musings be trusted as the thoughts of a philosopher? What does it mean for a philosopher to speak amid the sumptuous and sensuous arousals and carousals of Latin American dance and samba? What is the nature of the philosophical voice, the disembodied voice that purports to express the truth, devoid of rhetoric and ploy? What does it mean for a philosopher to adorn a kimono and play with his femininity with coquettish flair and poise? What does it mean for him to wander amid the poor and dispossessed seeking a humanity stripped of formal rights, responsibilities, and legal contracts? Yet, again, perhaps this is still too harsh. To speak of the darkness of the cave is perhaps to speak metaphorically of the hither side of rationality, above and beyond the staid, death-in-life of the solitary-philosopher. It is to speak amidst the chaos and darkness, betwixt the cadences, shrieks, and coos of the animal kingdom and the baying of blood and throbbing of the heart.

Thitherto, for a philosopher to perform as Lingis does, in the material and performative mode would be to risk ridicule. He is indeed an experimenter! Yet, perhaps therefore a different kind of philosophy is at work, for this is a philosophy which incorporates phenomenological description, anthropology, psychoanalysis, sociology, as well as anecdote and personal observation. He writes both of the *non-places* of the world and of sites of authentic human communication. In the non-places of the world, amidst the rumble of the world of work and reason, across the transnational, gleaming, technocratic-commercial archipelago of urban technopoles,[7] Lingis notices the art of ignoring, the seeing without looking. Lingis finds in the network of non-places a fundamental non-communication. Intent on exploring the dark side of globalisation, those places and anonymous spaces through which one passes without communication, he forges a dualistic philosophy which differentiates the rational, Western, universal, Enlightenment societies of advanced planetary capitalism with mystical, religious societies, those Othered communities of difference.

Serres

One communes to become an other for the other, for the interlocutor. Serres' neo-Socratic theory is a model of the polis and police.[8] In the ideal metropolis of rational community and communication, the paragon is the phantasmagoria of harmonious dialogic, the purging of noise. The theory maps a milieu in which digitally encoded information and data is instantly graspable and where the equivocal voice of the outsider is jammed. In the ideal republic, Serres claims that communication is indeed possible as the 'I' and other are trained to code and decode meaning by using the same key.[9] Communication is the said, the dematerialised, rendered ethereal.

In searching for a theory—an ethical theory—outside the confines of information science and beyond a model of the simple exchange of messages, Lingis critically reads the search to expunge the world of noise and the parasite. For Lingis, communication is phenomenologically the exposure of oneself to the other. He considers the thither side of the sharing and decoding-recoding of the same key to expose the underside of the *a priori* sense of what is held in common. In his brilliant work *The Community of Those Who Have Nothing in Common*, Lingis critiques Serres' idea of noise and the view that the *parasite* of noise is an obstacle to communication. Lingis makes a fundamental distinction between the rational community and the community of those who have nothing in common. As he says:

> Anyone who thinks we are only emitting noise is the one who does not *want* to listen. The one who understands is not extracting the abstract form out of the tone, the rhythm, and the cadences—the noise internal to the utterance, the cacophony internal to the emission of the message. He or she is also listening to that internal noise—the rasping or smouldering breath, the hyperventilating or somnolent lungs, the rumblings and internal echoes—in which the message is particularized and materialized and in which the empirical reality of something indefinitely discernible, encountered in the path of one's own life, is referred to and communicated.[10]

In the latter, all are strangers for each other. However, such a community is the one which may appear from time to time in the non-places of the world of which Marc Augé writes,[11] as it is in the language of the latter community when breakdown occurs that we evince a language of responsibility—a veritable ethical and political language—which enables the interlocutor to speak in a singular voice. The non-places of which Augé writes are populated with dividuated impersons who by their very nature pursue the goals set by the world of work and reason. It is in the Heideggerian moment, according to Lingis, when the facade of the everyday erodes, the singular voice speaks, must speak, and must be heard.

For Lingis, in the ideal republic—the city of communication maximally purged of noise—universal, unequivocal communication would assume the form a transparent, albeit machinic, intersubjectivity. He reads Serres as positing the paragon of unequivocal communication as crystallised in the case of two modems, transmitting and receiving information-bits simultaneously.

The community in which one has nothing in common interrupts the rational community, the world of work and reason. Contra such interference and confusion, interlocutors unite against those intent on scrambling communication. The one who speaks in his own name, in the first person singular, denudes himself or herself in the exposure to the other. As Lingis explains: "It is to risk what one found or produced in common."[12] In the rational community, people speak as agents or representatives of the common discourse. They engage in *serious speech* which conveys the imperative that determines what is to be said.[13] The voice is of the rational community, but it is not a singular voice. In the community of those who have nothing in common I speak for myself as a stranger, an outsider, as a newcomer. As Lingis says, I find my own voice and words which only I can singularly enunciate. It is in the act of enunciating the singular that I expose myself as a unique individual. I am at once exposed, vulnerable, and sensitive to the other. I engage in a language of responsivity and responsibility. Of singular importance for Lingis here is the response and the responsibility we assume.

Yet, Lingis takes exception to the argument that in some sense the authentic *sayable* of the said is external or outside the loop of information exchange, and transgressive of the incessant transmitting of messages. Critical of computer technology and the military for informing contemporary communication theory, Lingis counters this view by contending that what we often say to one another makes so little sense. "So little of it makes any pretence to be taken seriously, so much of it is simple malarkey, in which we indulge ourselves with the same warm visceral pleasure that we indulge in belching and passing air."[14]

Elsewhere, commenting on the nature of cues, watchwords, and passwords, Lingis makes the point equally well. Writing in Michael Strysick's *The Politics of Community*, Lingis claims: "So much of that language is non-serious or nonsensical. Greetings, hailing or confirming whatever the other is doing or saying, and jokes, teasing, and banter—much of the talk that goes on among us does not aim at truth but provokes smiles and laughter. Whoever laughs with us—or weeps with us—is one of us."[15]

In probing the *talk* and the idle chatter of *das gerede*—the talk which passes for communication, Lingis interprets the will to eliminate noise as a plot to eliminate the other, a xenophobic plot to eviscerate the other. As he says, communication is an effort to silence not the other, the interlocutor, but the outsider: the barbarian.[16]

BATAILLE AND COMMUNITY

In a similar vein to Deleuze and Guattari, Lingis's melding of phenomenology of the speculations on the nature of the singular is not for a contemporary readership, it is for those yet to come. He writes for those who seek experiences and ecstasy away from the classroom where students identify and assimilate information, away from the workplace and factory and the regulation of clock time. Thinking takes place among the poor and destitute, in places distant from the comfortable and suburban lives in developed countries. In *Dangerous Emotions*,[17] Lingis says that to lead comfortable and suburban lives is *to skim over reality*. As Lingis says in an essay *Joy in Dying*: "Heroes are those who live and die in high mountains and remote continents far from our comfortable and secure rooms in the urban technopoles, where we meet to read to one another what we have thought out on our computers."[18]

Embracing elements of Bataille's solar economy of expenditure without return, communication is perceived as functional, transgressive of the rational order of discourse. The mode of communication of value for Lingis is that which pertains to hæcceity or singularity. In the exclamations, cries, and guffaws of laughter, nothing is reciprocated. This is expenditure without return. There is a waste of energy. Nothing is exchanged. Outside the rational economy of equilibrium, Lingis says it is among those who we have nothing in common that we expose ourselves to expenditure, loss, and sacrifice. We find this sense of the nothing beyond exchange in *Contact and Communication*, when Lingis says: "This beyond is from the first empty; it is the void, nothingness."[19] The desire for communication breaks open the self-sufficiency of a sovereign being, her autonomy, her integrity, and opens her upon something beyond herself. To communicate with another then is to break through integrity, independence, autonomy, and nature. It is to intrude, unsettle, and wound. Lingis says that community forms a movement by which one exposes oneself to the other, to forces and powers outside oneself, "to death and to the others who die."[20] What we bear witness to is the inapprehensible, the inassimilable, and the irrecuperable. We can think of Bataille's theory of 'unemployed negativity' as a collapsing of the work, of *l'oeuvre*. It is the non-productive. Jean-Luc Nancy derives the concept of the inoperable community from Bataille. The inoperable implies a sense of worklessness and idleness (*désoeuvrement*). It is a community nonproductive of itself.[21] Lingis takes from Nancy the notion of distress and asks how knowledge is gained through the coexistence with the other. To understand Lingis's theory of communication it is important to appreciate how distress in the outer zones becomes our distress. He inquires into the shared sense of distress when we become cognisant of the "exterminations wrought upon peoples in and also the culture of technicization and simulation that reigns in the richest urban technopoles."[22] If the outer zone is the site of the sacred, then Lingis is a philosopher of the outer zone, a philosopher of the sacred.

Lingis thinks contact with the other as constitutive of a fundamental communication that is literally destructive. At stake in the risk of communication is a violation and decomposition of the integrity of the body; a collapse of self-possession and self-positing subjectivity, a loss of control. In fact, a base communication and materialism demands a destratification of identity, or according to Bataille, a sovereignty without mastery. Communication implies moments in individuals when sovereignty is neither autonomy nor domination over others; it is a state individuals find in themselves. It is through contamination and contact with alterity, in a relation of exposure and abandon, that communication takes place. One cannot appropriate the sovereignty of the other through communication. On the contrary, it is the giving without return, a fusion of subject and object. Identity with the other is through non-rational means in the sense of laughter, tears, or the erotic. Laughter and tears tear apart from the world of work and reason. And for Lingis, it is in laughter, tears and eroticism that we find the conditions of possibility for communication in rational, instrumental thought. Lingis finds in blessings and cursings a primary form of speech. Lingis writes: "Laughter and tears, blessing and cursing break through the packaging and labeling of things that make our environment something only scanned and skimmed over. They are the forces with which we impact on nature, which we had perused only as the text of the world. They are forces that seek out and engage reality."[23] Humans through blessings and curses—as instances of fundamental modes of language and community—converse over that which is amusing or tormenting.

Contra Kant, Lingis is sceptical of the universal rational agent and the law of the categorical imperative which set examples for everyone. Contrary to the notion that the rational agent respects the other via respect for the law that rules and binds, Lingis finds in Bataille an alternative model in which communication pertains not to the contract but to the contact of an individual with what is and remains beyond him. Sovereignty is ridiculous. It is a danger. For Lingis, the communication of sexual pleasure comes closest to the essence of majesty. It is through the intermingling of bodies that we come to know the other. Lingis finds in Bataille the idea that communication pertains to the contact of a sovereign being with what is other, a communication with the sacred and demonic and a communication with other species, inanimate things, and the material universe: an ecology.[24] Yet the anxiety that composes it is speechless.

For Lingis, the thirst for communication is for contact with beings unlike ourselves. He argues that humans seek communication with those different from themselves. And in more exotic terms, he writes: "Our most important conversations are with prostitutes, criminals, gravediggers. We seek to be freed from the carapace of ourselves."[25] Beyond the world of work and reason, Lingis thinks the outer zone, the world of the other, the world of the sacred. Seemingly uninterested in the world of abstract, disembodied thought and the profane sphere of everyday existence, Lingis speaks of the time of the sacrificial and the mystical. Here perhaps is the secret to understanding Lingis. If the sacred is the zone of the decomposition of the world of work and reason, and if following his reading Bataille, we find the most sacred things in the spilling of bodily fluid, then we can take Lingis as saying that the deep-seated and ancient sense of communication is the longing to communicate with those most unlike ourselves—

with sacred and demonic beings. Then, it would seem that Lingis's theory of communication is a theory of communication of the sacred. Lingis understands those who perform sacrifice as the true identifiers with the victim. It is through wounds that communication takes place between humans and sacred beings. One is exposed to the others by wounds. Moreover, for Lingis following Bataille, communication with the sacred and with natural things is in some sense prior to communication with other humans. At a more fundamental level, communication takes places between human beings when we share laughter, grief, and erotic feelings, when dignity is punctured.

> To communicate effectively with those who fascinate us is to break through their integrity, their natures, their independence, their autonomy—to wound them.[26]

For Lingis, sovereign existence is lived in conversations, shared laughter, friendship, and eroticism. Indeed, fundamental truths are revealed in laughter, friendship, and eroticism. It is in moments of conversation and laughter, in perversity in all its myriad forms that we live a sovereign existence. And it is precisely when we laugh together that humans recognise each other as the same kind, as kindred. In similar ways, we know one another as human through our tears, and through the sexual appetite and attraction. At the limit of communication and community is the 'nothing-in-common' through which communication takes place. This is the moment of unemployed negativity that we find in Bataille.

ORDER-WORDS

In *A Thousand Plateaus*,[27] Deleuze and Guattari consider slogans or order-words (*mots d'ordre*) in non-ideological terms. Interpreted as such, they are the cues, prompts, watchwords, and passwords which we attach and avail ourselves to as representatives of this or that discipline, body, or group. For Deleuze and Guattari, the talk or indirect discourse communicates what someone has heard and what someone has been told to say. Order-words command the informative content of sentences. Deleuze and Guattari perceive obedience as the honouring of order-words. In speaking to others, we transmit to them what we have been told to say.

In the anti-Chomskyian linguistic thrust of Deleuze and Guattari, a positive emphasis is put on fleeing their inherent command. While acknowledging the forlornness in seeking to escape order-words, Lingis, echoing Deleuze and Guattari, claims the trick is to escape the death sentence and the verdict they contain. Such order-words are a "verdict"—a "death sentence."[28] Yet Lingis is interested in how the 'I' speaks in its own name. He says that this will to disclose is not derived from a moment of Heideggerian authenticity but is forged through a collective, a social machine that compels the 'I' to speak in its own name. And in doing so blocks other paths of creativity and flight, for order-words isolate "an inner core of lucidity and will," and excise a "swarming within of becomings—becoming woman, becoming animal, becoming vegetable, rhizomatic, becoming mineral, becoming molecular."[29] For Lingis, to speak in one's own name is to disconnect from a vital environment. To delimit one's possibilities is a process of subjectification, a subjection and subjugation.[30]

Conclusion

Lingis writes from the perspective of the 'I,' from the singular, from the perspective of saying things simply in one's own name as Nietzsche exhorted his readers to do. He probes the 'I's relation and bond with the *l'autrui*, the other, and explores why it is that we understand so little of the other. We might say that his linguistic theory is liminally orientated as it contests what can be said or not—it addresses limits of the sayable in words and thoughts. He thinks the outside of language, the unsayable, the non-rational and unrepresentable and transgressive. In a sense, he searches for the compulsions to act and speak. As a phenomenological archaeologist of desire, he suggests there are communications more profound than the babble of the everyday, the talk of *the they*. He beseeches his readers to consider the traumatising question 'are you everyday?'

---

[1] Alphonso Lingis, "Emanations," *Parallax* 16.2 (2010): 15–16.
[2] Alphonso Lingis, "Our Uncertain Compassion," *Janus Head* 9.1 (2006): 27.
[3] Alphonso Lingis, *The Imperative* (Bloomington: Indiana University Press, 1998), 180.
[4] Alphonso Lingis, "Defenestration," paper delivered at Deleuze Conference: "On Media and Movement," University of California, Berkeley, November 3, 2006.
[5] Emmanuel Levinas, *Totality and Infinity: An Essay on Exteriority*, trans. Alphonso Lingis (Pittsburgh: Duquesne University Press, 1969.
[6] Emmanuel Levinas, *Collected Philosophical Papers*, trans. Alphonso Lingis (The Hague: Martinus Nijhoff, 1987).
[7] Sheppard, Darren, Simon Sparks, and Colin Thomas, eds., *On Jean-Luc Nancy: The Sense of Philosophy*. (London: Routledge, 1997), 190.
[8] Michel Serres, *Hermes: Literature, Science, Philosophy*, eds. Josué V. Harari and David F. Bell (Baltimore: Johns Hopkins University Press, 1982).
[9] Alphonso Lingis, *The Community of Those Who Have Nothing in Common* (Bloomington: Indiana University Press, 1994), 65.
[10] Lingis, *The Community of Those Who Have Nothing in Common*, 91.
[11] Marc Augé, *Non-Places: Introduction to an Anthropology of Supermodernity* (London: Verso, 2006).

[12] Lingis, *The Community of Those Who Have Nothing in Common*, 87.

[13] Lingis, *The Community of Those Who Have Nothing in Common*, 112.

[14] Lingis, *The Community of Those Who Have Nothing in Common*, 104.

[15] Michael Strysick, Michael, *The Politics of Community* (Aurora, CO: Davies Group, 2002).

[16] Lingis, *The Community of Those Who Have Nothing in Common*, 97.

[17] Alphonso Lingis, *Dangerous Emotions* (Berkeley: University of California Press, 2000), 79.

[18] Lingis, *Dangerous Emotions*, 164.

[19] Andrew J. Mitchell and Jason Kemp Winfree, eds., *The Obsessions of Georges Bataille: Community and Communication* (Albany: SUNY Press, 2009), 122.

[20] Lingis, *The Community of Those Who Have Nothing in Common*, 12.

[21] Jean-Luc Nancy, *The Inoperative Community*, trans. Peter Connor, Lisa Garbus, Michael Holland, and Simona Sawhney (Minneapolis: University of Minnesota Press, 1991).

[22] Nancy, *The Inoperative Community*, 190.

[23] Lingis, *Dangerous Emotions*, 78

[24] For more on Lingis's idea of ecology in relation to blessing see Lingis, *Dangerous Emotions*, 71: "A thinker who comprehends with the hands, hands made for blessing, sees swallows and owls, wetlands and tundra pullulate with grace. Blessing is the beginning and the end of all ecological awareness."

[25] Lingis, *Dangerous Emotions*, 101.

[26] Lingis, *Dangerous Emotions*, 101.

[27] Gilles Deleuze and Félix Guattari, *A Thousand Plateaus: Capitalism and Schizophrenia*, trans. Brian Massumi (Minneapolis: University of Minnesota Press, 1987).

[28] Deleuze and Guattari, *A Thousand Plateaus*, 107.

[29] Alphonso Lingis, "Subjectification," *Continental Philosophy Review* 40.2 (2007): 115.

[30] Lingis, "Subjectification," 116.

On *The Community of Those Who Have Nothing in Common*[1]

by Jeffrey Nealon

A note from the author about the following text: This is an archival text, delivered at a Penn State Philosophy Department session on Al's book in 1995, shortly after it had been published. Despite my desires to change, update, and fudge, I preserve the original discourse in accordance with what I learn from Lingis's example—the difficult joy of response, the irreducible singularity of the encounter, and the liveliness of memory, among so many other things.

I find myself in a somewhat odd position here this afternoon, having been charged with the task of "briefly reviewing the main ideas" of Alphonso Lingis's truly remarkable book, *The Community of Those Who Have Nothing in Common*. The difficulty, I guess, is two-fold. First is the problem that one encounters before any such rich and engaging text, the uncomfortable difficulties of paraphrase: Have I gotten it right? Are these really the stakes of the project, or am I just making this up? How to impart a sense of the text's rich complexity, while still performing some kind of recognizable summary?

And then there's the second problem—the fact that Al is sitting right here, across the table from me, face-to-face. I'm thinking he could review the main ideas for us a lot better than I could, so what do you need me for, I begin to wonder? But I press on, trying to find a path, as we always do in Al's work, for productively engaging the joyously cramped space of response.

One is tempted, in confronting these initial difficulties, to introduce the book by situating it within an ongoing scholarly conversation. And Lingis's book certainly does intervene decisively among a series of recent philosophical works that take up the question of community from a continental perspective—most notably, Jean-Luc Nancy's *The Workless Community*, Maurice Blanchot's *The Unavowable Community*, William Corlett's *Community Without Unity*, and Derrida's *The Other Heading: Reflections on Today's Europe*; in turn, these books expand on certain themes of alterity and community articulated by Heidegger, Levinas, Bataille, and others. Then, of course, there is also much work on community that comes out of Hegelian, Marxist, and postcolonial traditions—say, Charles Taylor's work or Habermas's or Fanon's—and one could perhaps introduce Lingis's work by situating it within the debates among communitarianism, Marxism, and postcolonial studies.

However, as tempting as it is, such scholarly situating will never get to the heart and singularity of a work like Lingis's. Even from within the attempt to convene a community of works on community, I am inexorably thrown back on the difficult question of responding adequately to *this* work, to *The Community of Those Who Have Nothing in Common*. Its specificity calls *not* for comparison to a community of other works, but rather for a radically singular response.

Of course, maybe this isn't such a big deal, insofar as this type of problem is confronted and eventually overcome all the time, in any successful philosophical discussion of a theme within a community of like-minded inquirers. Something like this difficulty, in fact, is *issue one* in many scholarly studies of community: How does one adequately respond to the rich complexity of alterity while still building the rational consensus necessary for mutual discussion and progress? How does one begin to form a *community* out of a bunch of people who have *nothing in common*? As Lingis himself writes on this model, "To build community would mean to collaborate in industry which organizes the division of labor and to participate in the market. It would mean to participate in the elaboration of a political structure, laws and command posts. It would be to collaborate with others to build up public works and communications" (5). These are certainly pressing, difficult themes, and ones that could potentially occupy us in discussion for quite some time this afternoon. We could debate, for example, whether it really *does* take a village to raise a child.

However, an *other*, more essential, difficulty is presented to us by *The Community of Those Who Have Nothing in Common*: from the beginning, this text is not primarily interested in philosophical discussions—in the progress of knowledge or the parsing deliberation of arguments; it's not interested in founding a rational community based on the properly communicated abstraction or the triumphant conclusion. Rather, the stakes of *The Community of Those Who Have Nothing in Common* lie irreducibly elsewhere.

At the same time, Lingis's text most certainly *is* concerned with communication and community; it just asks us to consider a communication that happens or community that forms around situations *other* than the rational exchange of information within a community of like-minded individuals. As he writes, "Beneath the rational community . . . is another community, the community that demands that the one who has his own communal identity, who produces his own nature, expose himself to the one with whom he has nothing in common, the stranger. The *other community* is not simply absorbed into the rational community; it recurs, it troubles the rational community, as its double or its shadow" (10).

It is, then, toward this other community—the community before, beneath, or beyond the rational community of progress and consensus—that Lingis relentlessly draws our attention. In a sentence that might be said to mark the book's most insistently recurring gesture, Lingis writes that "Before the rational community, there was the encounter with the other" (10). And, for Lingis, this kind of encounter with the other is one that necessarily takes place *both inside and outside* the dominant laws and norms of any given political culture; such an encounter demands that we respond to the other, without any concrete sense of how we might adequately render such a response. As he puts it, "To respond to the other, even to answer her greeting, is already to recognize her rights over me. Each time I meet his glance or answer her words, I recognize that the imperative that orders his or her approach commands me also. I cannot return her glance, extend my hand, or respond to his words without exposing myself to his or her judgment and contestation" (33).

As Lingis shows throughout his text, much "philosophical" discussion of community unfortunately boils down to a series of questions concerning how one can *overcome* difference—how a community can put its differences aside and work together toward common goals, in the project of forming what Hegel famously calls the "I that is We and We that is I." For Lingis, however, the I or the subject is related less to a common "We" [W-E] than it is a singular *oui* [O-U-I], to an imperative saying-yes to alterity. This yes, this other *oui*, cannot merely be understood as a rational or normative rule of the community's law; as he writes, "It is not only with one's rational intelligence that one exposes oneself to an imperative" (11); rather, as Lingis shows us through the many interventions and encounters in his text, the imperative to respond to the other shows itself and becomes compelling precisely at the *limits* of the rational community—at those places or in those moments where the *content* of *what we say* is less important than the raw, phatic fact of speaking, being-there, accompanying the other, responding to the other's approach, answering the other's call.

Lingis thematizes this distinction between two kinds of communications, two communities, as follows: "There are then two entries into communication—the one which depersonalizes one's visions and insights, formulates them in the terms of the common rational discourse, and speaks as a representative, a spokesperson—equivalent and interchangeable with others—for what has to be said. *The other entry into communication is that in which you find it is you, you saying something, that is essential*" (116). This speaking other-wise is the radically singular *saying* that comes before the general or translatable *said* of rational communication; such saying is, then, literally the origin of community and dialogue, but it is itself not a generalizable or translatable component of rationalist discussion. The simple fact of my speaking in response to the approach of an other is already a testament to the other's primacy and irreducibility; but, as Lingis insists, "it is also a beginning, the beginning of communication" (114).

Throughout *The Community of Those Who Have Nothing in Common*, Lingis consistently calls our attention to these other entries into "communication" (or these entries into an *other* communication) at the margins of a community: encountering a stranger in a foreign land, our call to the bedside of a dying loved one, the caress in desire, our stammering confrontations with language. Such radically singular events mark "A situation in which the saying, essential and imperative, separates from the said, which somehow it no longer orders and hardly requires" (109). And it is, Lingis shows, precisely at these *limits* of communication—at those moments when response is always necessary, yet always irrational and out of our control—that communication itself is born.

As he writes, it is "the *surfaces* of the other, the surfaces of suffering, that face me and appeal to me and make demands on me. In them, an alien imperative weighs on me. The weight of the imperative is felt in the surfaces with which the other faces me with his weariness and vulnerability and which afflict me and confound my intentions" (32). Communication begins or happens, in other words, *not* when I confidently transfer my abstract meaning or ideas to the other, but rather in those moments when my self-assured projects falter, where my spontaneity is called radically into question by the sheer presence of the other. Such limit-experiences comprise an irrecoverable movement outside the self, a gesture that "has no idea of what to do or how to escape. Its movement is nowise a project; one goes where one cannot go, where nothing is offered and nothing is promised" (178). Such a gesture of response, in other words, moves inexorably toward the exterior, toward the other.

There certainly is, then, a surviving notion of community in Lingis's text—a quite literal community of those who have nothing in common—but such a community is formed *not* by a closing in, by the issuing of ID cards or by the creation of a common interior space, safe from irrational intrusion; rather, Lingis holds that "Community forms in a movement by which one exposes oneself to the other, to forces and powers outside oneself, to death and to the others who die" (12).

In the end, it seems to me that Lingis's interventions into the discourses of community are essentially ethical interventions; both the philosophical stakes and—just as importantly—the metonymic or empirical operations of the surface of his text comprise powerfully compelling ethical movements. However, the ethical component of this text is *not* to be found in abstract systems of reciprocal obligation; rather, ethics in *The Community of Those Who Have Nothing in Common* is born and maintained through the continuing necessity of *response*—to other people, to animals, to the earth itself. And such a responsiveness or responsibility comes always *before* and *beyond* the solidification of any theoretical rules or political norms of ethical conduct. This is why, throughout the text, Lingis consistently calls us to consider the primacy of what we might call "non-philosophical" experience—that is, he continually calls attention to the primacy of an experience of sociality or otherness that comes before any philosophical understanding or reification of our respective subject positions.

In this insistence, perhpas we see Lingis's debt to Levinas's (non)concept of the "face-to-face" encounter with the other. As Levinas writes, in Lingis's translation, the face-to-face "situation is an experience in the strongest sense of the term: a contact with a reality that does not fit into any a priori idea, which overflows all of them. . . . A face is pure experience, conceptless experience."[2]

In Lingis's work, like Levinas's, such an "experience" exceeds all my categories of knowledge or understanding. This relation between self and other cannot simply be translated into rational, conceptual thought, because to do so would be to destroy the unmotivated, spontaneous character of encounter. But, at the same time, there is an obligation to respond built into the very situation of the face-to-face encounter, insofar as the experience of the other person is also a concrete, social phenomenon. As Lingis writes, "The face of the other is the original locus of expression" (63), and we must respond to this social fact of otherness just as we must respond to the experiential fact that fire burns flesh or food nourishes it; such response does not simply—or even primarily—find its origin in the subject's "choice."

Ethics is born(e), then, not in the time of the community's progress—in the reciprocity of offers or promises made to the others—but rather in the time of the other, which Lingis calls "an utterly alien time where nothing is offered or promised" (178). All of my possibilities and enjoyments are, from the beginning and in the end, owed to the other. As Lingis writes near the end of his text, "For me, the world is, from the start, a field of possibilities others have apprehended and comprehended, possibilities for others. What I find as possibilities for me are possibilities others have left me" (177).

And, in, or at the end, it is just such a gift—a toolbox of possibilities for becoming-other—that Alphonso Lingis leaves *for us*, in the pages of his extraordinary *Community of Those Who Have Nothing in Common*.

Thank you, Al. Really.

---

[1] Alphonso Lingis, *The Community of Those Who Have Nothing in Common* (Bloomington: Indiana University Press, 1994); hereafter referred to parenthetically by page number.
[2] Emmanuel Levinas, "Philosophy and the Idea of Infinity," in *Collected Philosophical Papers*, trans. Alphonso Lingis (Pittsburgh: Duquesne University Press, 1987), 59.

What Is an Imperative?

by Dorothea Olkowski

THE VORTICES

Each morning we wake up to an ongoing miracle. Light is there for us and it forms a level. Along this level I see the color-contrasts of the Western mountain range's phosphoresce. Sounds awaken too. They awaken out of the level that is the murmur of nature from which the cry of hawks, the whining of coyotes fill the air. And close by, the harsh colored billboards stick up in the level of the light as the the cars and trucks roll by, hurried and noisy, emerging from the level that is sound, the sound of the strong winds blowing up a storm heading east to the plains where they meet the Gulf moisture, twisting it into tornadoes. These levels, as Alphonso Lingis calls them, "form *in a medium* without dimensions or directions: the luminosity more vast than any panorama that the light outlines in it, the vibrancy that prolongs itself outside the city and beyond the murmur of nature, the darkness more abysmal than the night from which the day dawns and into which it entrusts itself."[1]

This medium is the world, but how are we to characterize it, how to make sense of the way in which it gives rise to levels? And do we understand in what manner levels give rise, not only to competent bodies able to negotiate the practicalities of life, bodies for which seeing and seeing the true are one and the same, but also to all the rest, "the monocular phantasms, mirages, and depths of floating color and shadow, tonalities and scents, erotic obsessions, nocturnal phantasms, mythogenic and magical realms."[2] To the extent that we do not yet understand these things, we will begin by positing a world that is neither coherent nor incoherent, neither real nor imaginary.[3] Instead, in an *epoché*, a suspension of understanding and reason, even further removed from the subject than that of Henri Bergson, who asks us to begin our reflections on the world with nothing more than images, let us begin, following Lingis, with the sensible intuition of a world set in depths and uncharted abysses.[4]

In the world of depths and abysses, Lingis tells us, sensibility can be drawn in and drawn in *imperatively* to the *vortices* that populate these depths. In physics, vortices have been described variously as "*'the sinews of turbulence,'* [and] *'the voice of fluid motion.'*"[5] Unlike solids, which do not manifest vortices, "*'the essence of fluid is vortices,'*" especially insofar as fluids at rest cannot stand *shear stress*, the tendency of a fluid to be "pulled apart" (sheared) by a differential force.[6] Shear stress puts fluid elements into spinning motion, causing rotational or vortical flow.[7] Fluid motion produces vortices via the rotation of fluid elements. Vortices are manifest in spiral galaxies, hurricanes, tornadoes, and in the vortex rings of the mushroom cloud of a nuclear explosion.[8] Let us not assume however that the presence of a vortex signals the lack of a coherent structure. The study of vortices is central to understanding the functioning of aerodynamics, as well as to the understanding of the formation and evolution of large-scale vortices in the ocean and atmosphere, both of which play a crucial role in geophysical fluid dynamics.[9]

Such vortices, Lingis posits, are precisely what occur in

the depths of the world. Although they first form us, we find them only where the body lets loose its hold on the levels that provide perceptual consistency and coherence revealing "apparitions made of light, voices of the abyss, enigmas made of darkness."[10] Where Immanuel Kant posited a universe of three faculties: intuition, understanding, and reason, in which reason determines and makes intelligible the other two, and together, the three produce God, the World, and the Self, Lingis seems to turn the Kantian thesis on its head.[11] The universe—the world preexists our faculties and is the medium in which our sensibility first finds itself—first takes shape in the vortices of the world which is the medium that shapes our sensitivities and sensibilities and eventually shapes our understanding and our reason.

In the vortices of the medium, we are not in the realm of what can be done but in the realm of appearances where no *thing*, no object according to a concept, appears. It is the realm of phantoms, caricatures, doubles floating over the contours of things, and planes in the world.[12] And, of the utmost importance, it is the realm where the imperative first makes itself known to us as to all the phenomena of this world. The visionary eye obeys the imperative to shine, to light beyond every and any specified direction. Vertigo obeys the imperative to deepen endlessly. Hearing obeys the imperative to become vibrant beyond every and any situation. And eventually, all phenomena obey the imperative to let go of the world forever, to become elemental, returning to the vortices out of which all things and beings emerge.[13]

No longer maintaining ourselves, letting loose our hold on things, un-holding the levels that give us a grip on the world transports "us" or what is left of "us" to an infantile and phantasmal existence wherein other bodies materialize as forces and powers that belong to enigmatic imperatives without which our world is nothing but tasks, objectives, competence, and agency.[14] But what is it that we let loose of, what grip do we have on the world and things, or is it that the world and things have a grip on us? To understand this, let us examine the idea of levels.

THE LEVELS

When we pass from light as immersion in radiance to light as it penetrates space, outlines contours, rests on surfaces, the light has become a level. We see according to the level that is the light leading us to things, just as we hear a piece of music according to the dominant chord when the band or orchestra begins to play.[15] Likewise, smell or taste function only in a medium of odors or tastes, just as everything touchable forms a level of pattern, grain, smoothness, hardness, softness—all of this taking place in a temporal level that directs our movements, visibility, resonance, looking, listening, touching.[16] Thus, levels—according to which we perceive—are purely *sensory phenomena* and for this reason impossible to measure and difficult even to conceptualize.

All the particulars of our sensory organs take place on the levels. Sounds, colors, tastes, contacts are not properties of things nor ideas of agents but characteristics acquired in relation to a level. As such they are "salients, contours, contrasts, inceptions and terminations," and as sensible characteristics, they play diacritically in the levels where they appear.[17] Thus the red flower invades the light and contrasts with it, it *greens* the leaves on the stem and *whitens* the sheets of the hospital room where it appears.[18] Unlike the Kantian object, which appears in the mathematical grid of the a priori space-time manifold, determined by a concept, and delimited by reason's rational order, "the sensory flux does not present itself as so many space-time points successively filled and emptied and filled again, but as a sphere in which points pivot, edges extend levels, spaces open paths, colors intensify themselves by playing across a field, tones thicken and approach and thin out and recede and send their overtones into one another."[19]

When this happens, when there is no a priori space-time manifold, then it seems that the contours of a figure do not take shape, a visible goes unseen, a sound unheard, a substance is not felt. Yet that is precisely when the sensorial medium called a level persists and asserts itself as a *directive that weighs on us*. It is a directive to us to mobilize! Our look is led by the directive, but we must focus and move our eyes. The music takes shape for us only when we start to dance; and to feel soft or hard surfaces, we must move our fingers and hands and adjust our bodies so as to hold our arms in the right position. Sensations take form in the vortices, but we must conduct our moves in accordance with their characteristics.[20] The visible, audible, and tangible unfold in the field even in mirages, in pianissimo, grazing our skin, for our bodies are such that they can "catch on" to even the slightest sensations and transmit motions to the entire body. So we sing *as* we swing our arms and turn our heads in the direction and rhythm of the music. In our bodies, nothing is isolated, everything is transmitted from one muscle to another as we follow the directives, the *imperatives* coming to us from the levels.

It is these directives, these imperatives, that are also the basis of our coexistence, our community with others. Long before we engage with the understanding and the reasoning faculty of others, we come upon one another in the levels of sensibility, the elements that direct us as we sense sentient bodies seeing and touching in the levels, accompanying us, our sensibilities displaced into those others, and theirs also onto ours, variants of one another.[21] Their ears hear what we hear so that when we have left the room, the forest, the oceanside, and they stay, the levels, the sensory elements, the reliefs and contours, the sonorities and tangibilities that direct them and us remain operative, so sight, hearing, touch, smell all continue, open to directing all of us, should we return.

Given the elemental nature of levels that provide directives, it makes sense that things call to our bodies so profoundly. "A perceived this is a pole which draws the convergent surfaces and organs of our bodies like a telos, a task. The reality of things is not given in our perception, *but orders it as in imperative.*"[22] It is not we who judge the intelligibility of things but things that "try out their reality in indecisive and inconclusive appearances."[23] Recent studies in the physiology of perception indicate that when sensory messages are available, chaotic, collective activity involving millions of neurons is essential to rapid recognition. What is relevant here is that when cortical neurons are *excited*, their output increases until they reach a maximal rate. If, for example, an odorant is active such that the neuronal collectives are generally aroused, the information spreads "like a flash fire through the nerve cell assembly.... so that the input rapidly ignites an explosion of collective activity throughout the entire assembly," spreading until it ignites a "full blown burst."[24] Such nearly instantaneous activity allows for novel activity patterns and implies that the brain seeks information.

Adapted to Lingis's model, we may say that the imperative to seek information comes not only from the "brain," but initially from the levels, from the environment of things. Things are not dead matter. They push back and push aside other things and "clamor for our attention" as our senses sink into the depths of things, not content to remain on the surface.[25] This is why Lingis states that on the levels of sensuality, the levels along which we move, our enjoyment is not distinctly our own, but the night, the light, the air, the earth are all *depersonalizing*. Everything open to us is first open to others, open to anyone in their range with the ability to perceive or use them.[26]

Thus, language is not first. Language, the symbolic realm, is not the first medium of communication.[27] The ability to use concepts, to reason about space or time, the ability to universalize our acts such that any one, at any time, in equivalent circumstances would act in the same way, none of these are the basis of our communication with and affinity for others. Rather, wherever we go, whatever we perceive, someone else has been there first and their inhabitation of that level and its perceptibles will inevitably have entered that level and will inform our engagement with that level and whatever things emerge in it.

FREE WILL

For Kant, the whole point of moral law is to free us from nature's causal forces. Newtonian science, with its laws of motion governing the motions of physical bodies, seemed to have made this a difficult goal. The possibility of what Kant calls "free will" is radically undermined. So we must think our way out of this. We *know* that we are causal phenomena in nature, but nevertheless, we *think* that we are free, that our actions are intelligent, that we do not follow blind impulse.[28] How is this done? Autonomy, freedom from nature's mechanical causality, which is to say, from our own bodily pleasures and pains, is taken to be an imperative. Although nature is mechanical, each subject feels its effects differently. Some like the feeling of beaches and ocean, others prefer cold mountain tops, but no one can remove themselves from some feeling, thus there is always a subjective incentive to choose one or another object.

If freedom means that there is an unconditioned first cause of our actions, then subjective preferences will not yield this; they remain subject to nature's causal forces. Yet, we do feel something that informs us that we are free. We feel the check on our self-love.[29] This feeling alerts us to the existence of freedom because we ask ourselves, what is it that is putting this check on self-love? We first examine our maxims of subjective desire and find only self-love there; so then we abstract from all empirical conditions, all particular objects and goals that are motivated by self-love. What we are left with is the form of giving the universal rule, freedom in the strictest, transcendental sense, the form of all possible imperatives to act. We harmonize this transcendental law with our subjective desires by checking inclinations, and we feel the pain of rejecting every sensible condition, every "I desire," leaving us, in the end, with the negative feeling which is respect for moral law, respect for our ability to cease to be subject to nature's mechanical causal forces. We abstract from our subjective inclinations leaving only objective rules for the will.

But subjective humiliation yields objective respect, the so-called a priori or intellectual feeling of respect for moral law, because it blocks subjective feeling, a block caused by our intellectual recognition of freedom from nature's causal mechanism.[30] The blockage, the pain, the humiliation, is the subjective, sensible incentive to never act on sensible, subjective motives and, therefore, to act only on the basis of freedom. This is what is called, by Kant, moral law. For the sake of freedom, all inclinations are limited, choked off. Our recognition of freedom constrains us, makes it a duty, a rule characterized by an "ought," that we ought not to act on subjective motives and that this law must completely determine the will, and not just mine, but everyone's, anyone who thinks.[31] When freedom alone determines the will, its laws are categorical imperatives; they are thus necessary, unconditional, free of inclinations, and thereby universal.[32]

It seems that Lingis agrees with Kant that an imperative is a practical necessity arising with and out of respect.[33] But as Lingis notes, for Kant, "the immediate effect of the rational activity of the will is the reduction of sensuous impulses and appetites to impotence."[34] Negatively, this is something like fear; positively, it is something like inclination, that is, respect for law. Kant's imperative, Lingis continues, constitutes a typology according to which the person is constrained in three ways. First, we are constrained to represent the sensible world as surface effects of bodily physiology and physiochemical natural forces. Second, we are constrained to view our sensory and motor powers as solely in the service of the the rational, practical faculty. And third, we are constrained to imagine ourselves as wholly obedient to the commands of reason.[35] And of course, the commands of reason, the law, is a set of properties drawn from logic, the logic that was validated by Newtonian physics.[36] But as Lingis points out, in the current era, mathematics and the logics utilized in mathematics make use of a vast array of idealized conceptual models. Mathematics is not unified but divided into a plethora of mathematical disciplines.[37] Thus, what is needed now is not representations of our nature, of our faculties as instrumental systems and ourselves as microsocieties, but something else, some other *imperative* that accounts for our sensuality, sensitivity, perception, thought, and motility.[38]

THE IMPERATIVE OF THE OTHER

Why something else, why another sort of imperative? Perhaps the urgency of this other imperative emerges for Lingis in the analysis of the other, which he formulates in terms borrowed from Emmanuel Levinas. Hands that touch others "do not move with their own goals in view; they are moved, troubled by the touch of the other with which they make contact, afflicted with the pleasure and the torment of the other."[39] The imperative is formulated in this manner because the hands now "make contact with a vulnerability that *summons them*, a susceptibility that *puts demands on them*."[40] So, it is the case here that the ethical imperative is not subjectively motivated, but neither is it a rational imperative to respect universal law. The imperative comes instead from the depth where vortices form levels according to which phenomena are perceived. "We greet the other as a depth structure of forces, and recognize community with him or her, in the handshake that seals the pact."[41]

Nevertheless, the sounds of wind or traffic or the sight of forests or cities is not the same as the encounter with others who speak and act, who look into our own eyes with their eyes, whose words call up or respond to one's own speaking and hearing. Without the other who speaks to me, gestures at me, looks into my eyes and acts in the world, without this other, I have no world. The imperative of the other, the demands of the other that are put on me, the appeals made to me are all necessities for me, indications that the world they inhabit is also the the world open to me. "For it is before the face of the other that I first entered speech."[42] And even if I interpret or identify the other, represent the other, that other—all those specific and unique others moving through the world, perceiving that way they perceive, inhabiting levels in the manner that they do this—contests my manner of perceiving and inhabiting, my manner of moving and seeing, my speech and actions. Not an other me but a persistence that challenges my speech and actions, my perceptions and movements. The gaze, the skin, the anxiety, the laughter, the arrogance, the suffering, the age, the voice, the gait, the vulnerability, all belong to the other, all contest me with their very existence. This is now the sense of the imperative. It "weighs on us with the force of exteriority," such that we cannot but look, touch, caress or torment, except as an answer to the demand, the imperative to attend to the other.[43]

Yet, the question remains as to whether or not this is enough, whether it is adequate or not. That is, is the imperative addressed to us in the face of the other adequate to promulgate respect—or is it not just as easy for us physically or economically, psychologically or politically to not respect the imperative that comes from the other? Will this keep us from harming and destroying the other, taking away their land, their children, their futures, and their pasts? And if not, then given the disintegration of the universal, rational moral law, then what now, what next?

---

[1] Alphonso Lingis, *Foreign Bodies* (New York: Routledge, 1994), 23 (italics added).

[2] Maurice Merleau-Ponty, *The Visible and the Invisible*, trans. Alphonso Lingis (Evanston: Northwestern University Press, 1968), 28. Lingis, *Foreign Bodies*, 22.

[3] Merleau-Ponty, *The Visible*, 40.

[4] Henri Bergson, *Matter and Memory*, trans. N.M. Paul and W.S. Palmer (New York: Zone Books, 1988), 17.

[5] Jie-Zhi Wu, Hui-Yang Ma, and Ming-De Zhou, *Vorticity and Vortex Dynamics* (Berlin: Springer, 2006), 1.

[6] Wu, Ma, and Zhou, *Vorticity and Vortex Dynamics*, 2; "Shear Stress," *Eric Weinstein's World of Physics*, http://scienceworld.wolfram.com/physics/ShearStress.html.

[7] Wu, Ma, and Zhou, *Vorticity and Vortex Dynamics*, 2.

[8] Wu, Ma, and Zhou, *Vorticity and Vortex Dynamics*, 1.

[9] Wu, Ma, and Zhou, *Vorticity and Vortex Dynamics*, 5.

[10] Lingis, *Foreign Bodies*, 23.

[11] Immanuel Kant, *The Critique of Pure Reason*, trans. Norman Kemp Smith (New York: St. Martin's Press, 1965).

[12] Lingis, *Foreign Bodies*, 23.

[13] Lingis, *Foreign Bodies*, 23–24.

[14] Lingis, *Foreign Bodies*, 24–25.

[15] Alphonso Lingis, *The Imperative* (Bloomington: Indiana University Press, 1998), 25.

[16] Lingis, *The Imperative*, 26.

[17] Lingis, *The Imperative*, 27.

[18] Lingis, *The Imperative*, 28.

[19] Lingis, *The Imperative*, 29.

[20] Lingis, *The Imperative*, 30–31.

[21] Lingis, *The Imperative*, 36–37.

[22] Lingis, *The Imperative*, 63.

[23] Lingis, *The Imperative*, 64.

[24] Walter J. Freeman, "The Physiology of Perception," *Scientific American* 264.2 (February 1991): 78–85. Freeman, like most cognitivists, emphasizes the activity of the "brain"; nevertheless, we can extrapolate from his perspective to Lingis's.

[25] Lingis, *The Imperative*, 69.

[26] Lingis, *The Imperative*, 125.

[27] Lingis, *The Imperative*, 127.

[28] Kant, *The Critique of Pure Reason*, A800–804, B828–832.

[29] Immanuel Kant, *The Critique of Practical Reason*, trans. Lewis White Beck (New York: Bobbs-Merrill, 1956), 74.

[30] Kant, *The Critique of Practical Reason*, 76–77.

[31] Kant, *The Critique of Practical Reason*, 18–19, 83.

[32] Kant, *The Critique of Practical Reason*, 19, 27.

[33] Lingis, *The Imperative*, 174–175.

[34] Lingis, *The Imperative*, 184.

[35] Lingis, *The Imperative*, 195.

[36] Lingis, *The Imperative*, 207. I have also discussed the idea of the logical basis of Kant's practical reason in chapter 4 of *The Universal (In the Realm of the Sensible)* (New York: Columbia University Press, 2007).

[37] Lingis, *The Imperative*, 208.

[38] Lingis, *The Imperative*, 211.

[39] Lingis, *Foreign Bodies*, 170–171.

[40] Lingis, *Foreign Bodies*, 171 (emphases added).

[41] Lingis, *Foreign Bodies*, 185.

[42] Lingis, *Foreign Bodies*, 169.

[43] Lingis, *Foreign Bodies*, 177.

Interview with Alphonso Lingis

by Jonas Skačkauskas

Vilnius, Lithuania — Februrary 2010

INTELLECTUAL BIOGRAPHY

JS: You graduated from the Jesuit Loyola University in Chicago, you defended a dissertation at the University of Leuven, where the Husserl Archives were founded. During your time in Europe you seem to have attended lectures by Jean-Paul Sartre, Jacques Lacan and maybe other Parisian figures. What was to you most important during these formative years?

AL: Leuven was where I really learnt philosophy. When I was an undergraduate, I did not have a good education. At Leuven it was a historical program, so we had to study each period. But it had an emphasis on contemporary philosophy. And students were mostly interested in contemporary philosophy. And I was also. I wrote my dissertation on Sartre and Merleau-Ponty. For me that was the beginning. When I wrote my dissertation, then I started really to understand something.

JS: And how about your undergraduate studies at Loyola?

AL: I forgot everything from there. That was not very good.

JS: It seems that you visited Paris for philosophy during your studies in Europe.

AL: After the studies at Leuven a few times I spent some summer time in Paris. And I heard there some lectures by Lacan, and Merleau-Ponty one time, Sartre two times.

JS: What was the impression of encountering these figures?

AL: Well, I had no real personal encounter. But I think it's true that all the great philosophers, that I had some idea what kind of men they are, I admired them. In my first year in America, when I came back to teach, Paul Ricoeur came and spoke at my university. And he stayed three or four days. I spent time with him. And I admired him very much; he was a marvellous man. And, you know, I heard stories about Sartre. And every story was pretty admirable. Sartre was very generous. He would easily give money to students and so on. I have an admiration for the big thinkers.

JS: Were you influenced in any way by the events of May '68?

AL: Definitely. In the United States. And I was in Paris in that summer, although it was already going down. To me it was a very intoxicating time.

JS: Did you have any clear vision of the philosophy you wanted to engage in after your bachelor or even doctoral studies? How did you discover Merleau-Ponty and Levinas?

AL: For a long time I concentrated on educating. I devoted myself to teaching, and every class I tried to teach different new books and so on. For a long time I thought I had no ideas of my own. And then, after a while, I began to realize that sometimes you can have, you know, small ideas. And I began to write an article after finishing a course, putting together a few small ideas. I thought I had no big system. And then, I think, I was influenced by Henri Birault from Paris, who came to Penn State while I was teaching. He would take these little sections from Nietzsche and just spend two or three hours talking about this one section. And he did not want students to talk about other sections or connections with other sections. And then the other influence I had was from British philosophy: Wittgenstein, Austin, and Bernard Williams—I liked them very much. Then I got the idea after a while that that was the kind of philosophy I really liked—that you take some concrete issue and try to see it in a new way. And for a long time that was what I did. I think that's what I still do. And then sometimes, after you had two or three of these things, you can see that they are connected and make a bigger idea out of that. That to me is the most valuable philosophy. The most valuable philosophy is not the philosophy that is some big principles and abstract generalizations, but when you study some concrete thing and see it in a new way or see it more deeply. I think that is what Foucault did and also Merleau-Ponty.

JS: But don't you get lost in empirical details having no abstract orientation? Is not there a danger of naïve empiricism?

AL: Right, you are certainly right. Well, we have in philosophies, like in phenomenology, we do have some general concepts. I guess the ideas about method and general concepts that I learned from phenomenologists, little by little I criticized them more and more. Just take one concept: In phenomenology you have the position that here is consciousness and here is everything else. And this is the fundamental division. And when you think about it, that's a very strange view of the universe. All the sciences are completely different. In biology and evolution the human mind is immersed in nature. So more and more I criticized this phenomenological division. And the other side of it is that phenomenology just starts with my own consciousness and what I can myself be aware of in my own mind. But you know, then I studied Whitehead. I think the thought I got was that consciousness depends on all kinds of other things in the body. There is a kind of response in the nervous system, in the cells, in the blood stream, and so on. And some consciousness is just the top of many levels. I would like to see philosophy approach more in that way.

Going back to your question concerning how I discovered the philosophy of Levinas. The first year I came back from graduate school and started to teach in the United States, Ricoeur visited. And I asked him what is new in philosophy. And he said, the most important thing was the book of Levinas. So immediately I bought it. And then a publisher invited me to translate it. That's how I discovered him. I was very enthusiastic.

JS: And how did the philosophy of Nietzsche become important to you?

AL: I have liked Nietzsche from the beginning, but he was not an important philosopher for me until later. So, this tradition of Nietzsche, Bataille, and Deleuze—that was a kind of continuation there. And that became very important to me. I became very, very interested in Bataille, maybe about fifteen or twenty years ago. I read some Bataille when I was a graduate student, but later I read the complete works and I was very enthusiastic and talked about it in a class. So it became very important. For me, these three thinkers are interconnected—Nietzsche, Bataille, and Deleuze. I suppose that the phenomenology of Merleau-Ponty and Heidegger and then these other three were for me the richest, the ones who gave me most.

NATURE

JS: I would like to ask about your conception of nature. It seems that nature is one of the most important themes in your philosophy (although most often you address it indirectly). It seems that you conceive the universe, nature, life itself in purely positive terms—as fullness, as abundance that lacks nothing. It seems that the ontology which makes negativity important or even fundamental is unacceptable to you. Am I right?

AL: On the last concept, that of negativity, I suppose I was influenced by Deleuze and then later by some thoughts from Bataille. But this is not only a specific theoretical point, but it's sort of my practice that I began to realize.

We could take this idea that's Nietzschean and Deleuzian. That throughout the history of philosophy one could say that life was conceived negatively. Naturally, it reaches its strongest development in Hegel. This is the idea that a living thing is a material system that develops lacks—there's evaporation, the system becomes hungry and thirsty. And it's these lacks that agitate the system. The reason that an organism moves and is released to the environment is that it is driven by needs and lacks. I think that the concept of an organism has pretty much dominated from the beginning. I suppose an alternative idea I found originally in Bataille, but it seems to me it is everywhere in science: that, on the contrary, a living organism is a dynamo that produces energy. It produces more energy than it needs to survive. And then later I began to think that most of our lacks are produced because we spend so much energy releasing excess energy. And most of us get hungry because we've gone walking in the mountains all day. And we did that because we had excess energy, we had energy to burn, to discharge. I think that the lacks are intermittent and superficial. The only reason that there is hunger is that there is a full organism that exists, and that the need is intermittent; it depends on the fullness of the organism.

And then I began to realize that, when I try to talk about things, I always try to find some very strong and very clear example. For example, when I talk about honour, people want me to talk about dishonour and disgrace. I always instinctively felt that you first have to understand honour. And it is only if we could get very clear about what honour is that we can begin to speak about dishonourable activities and so on. So I think in my practice I always tried to look at positive cases. And very often, when I finished talking about it, I was not interested in negative cases. It happens from time to time that people want to know about dishonour and, I guess, I never thought about it because I was not very interested in it. It was so interesting to talk about the sense of honour. Deleuze somewhere wrote that Nietzsche wanted to have totally positive and affirmative philosophy.

JS: You write in *The Community of Those Who Have Nothing in Common* that there is also an alienation from the elements. How does this happen?

AL: I don't think I have very many general ideas about it. There are probably a multitude of different ways and reasons for that. Last night there was a sort of thought in the air. Say, on the one hand, sometimes I get such a sense that the human race is so bellicose, so warlike. I mentioned that in Spain every little town had a wall around it. It was amazing. Especially now, you know, when we're accustomed to driving in the United States from one end to the other without barriers, without custodies. But on the other hand, I am much more impressed by the fact that people do get along with one another, and people really take pleasure in just being together. So the affirmative fact seems much more fundamental. I said this a little bit last night, too. It seems to me that a war is a kind of artificial construction. First, you have to have the whole bureaucracy and industry and then you have to have certain leaders who can create war. Wars don't happen just because people feel antagonistic to one another. Even if you have two different ethnic groups—say French and Germans—even if they hate one another, there is no war, unless you have this machine that's constructed to build the weapons and the factories, and the army. That seems to me kind of an artificial thing. Even to build an army—there's something sort of puzzling to me.

I remember, years ago I went to a museum, I think it was in Czechoslovakia. And I discovered that somewhere two thousand years ago, there was a great Moravian empire that had conquered a large area there. They waged wars, they expanded their territory, and then history covered them over and they were pretty much forgotten, until it was rediscovered recently that they even existed. And I remember standing in this museum and thinking to myself that these thousands of Moravians decided to go and kill people and a lot of them were killed. For what? For the Moravian Empire? It always seems to me such an artificial thing.

You know, at the beginning of my career there was the Vietnam War. And that occupied everybody and that occupied me very much. I tried to argue against this war in any possible way. And that's all we talked about for ten years. Fifty thousand American soldiers were killed. And something like two or three million Vietnamese people were killed. And I went to Vietnam, maybe about ten years after the war. It was very difficult, because on my passport the

U.S. government forbade me to go there. And so I went with a little group from Australia. And when I went there, I realised that nobody talked about Vietnam anymore. For ten years this was the most important issue in the United States. And we lost, and fifty thousand American soldiers died. And then, ten years later it's like it does not matter, Vietnam isn't that important. Finally, the United States says okay, you just do whatever you want to do and it does not matter to us. And then later there was a war again in Nicaragua. That was the big issue. And in the last ten years you never see in the paper anything about Nicaragua. So it is unimportant. Just in those two examples these wars depend on somebody constructing a very artificial machine. First of all, someone decides that this is strategically important for the United States. And then, secondly, someone constructs this whole ideology that they are terrible enemies. This was what happened in Iraq—the idea that Saddam Hussein was like Hitler and that he had to be destroyed. There was a whole artificial construction.

JS: Let us return to your phenomenology of nature, that you exposed most systematically in your book *The Imperative*.

AL: I was very impressed with Levinas. So there were two sides. On the one side, there was this phenomenological analysis of what it means to be faced by someone and the dimension of appeal and demand that is there. The theme of the face is original and a completely new contribution to philosophy. But I think the other side is what he says about the elements and substances and so on. And it was also completely interesting. I just recently have gone back to these issues.

But I think that more and more as years passed I became more and more critical about the theoretical framework of Levinas. On the one hand, he does a kind of constitutive phenomenology that says things are in some way constituted by manipulation and detaching them and taking them into the home and all that. This is what makes them into curious things. So that is a kind of leftover of Husserl, this idea of constitution of objects. So nature is quite absent in his philosophy. And then, he wants to find ethical experience only in the face of his confrontation with another human being. Anyhow, all this seems to me so limited. If it's true that I feel that hunger and need of another human being is a demand put on me, then it is also about other species. If I come upon an injured bird or deer in a path, it is exactly the same thing, it seems to me.

And then this theme of religion in there, of God in there—I had real theoretical problems with it. The simplest way I can say it is that for Levinas what is distinctive about the human being that looks at me is that the needs and demands are unending. He says that the more responsible you are, the more responsibilities you discover. There is a sort of infinite, unending succession of demands that are made on me by anyone who faces me. On the one hand, it's simply false. I mean, take a simple example. It's true that I have a responsibility for my child to take care of his needs that he cannot take care of himself. But the child wants to be independent. I mean, all the others in the universe are not dependent on me. They don't want to be. My child doesn't want me to be taking care of his needs all his life. And that goes back to the idea that we talked about earlier, the idea that a living organism is a dynamo that produces excess energy gratuitously.

And then the other part, that is theoretically incoherent, is that he wants to say that it is God, that it is the monotheist God, that it is one God who speaks, who is the source of demands on me in every face that looks at me. That concept reduces the singularity and the diversity of people, who face me with each time singular and distinctive needs and appeals.

That dimension I did not like.

Just to say it in a very general way, these two things I didn't like. I didn't like the constitutive phenomenology. Actually, this is the new thought I had a couple of weeks ago. It goes back to what I said of Merleau-Ponty a little bit and Whitehead. I mean, for constitutive phenomenology, and later for Derrida, the issue is that the world of my experience is in some way constituted by me. It's me who outlines and circumscribes things into things, makes them into things and then gives them meaning. And of course for Derrida it goes through the grid of language. But to me, you know, I have this very simple-minded objection from evolutionary psychology, that my experiences, my eyes are essentially similar to the eyes of other mammals. A cat or a fox sees the world as real things that exist in themselves, that are independent of them. That seems to me a very fundamental objection to every kind of idealism.

ETHICS

JS: It seems that your conception of ethics is closely linked or even deeply intertwined with the realm of nature. In *Dangerous Emotions* you talk about human animals being in a fundamental relationship with living and non-living nature. You write about our affinity with animals, describing how movements of our bodies, our emotions, pleasures, sexuality, and even virtues mimic theirs. Can you comment on your conception of ethics? Which philosophers were sources of inspiration for this conception?

AL: I suppose I came from two directions. From Levinas starting with the idea that I see the needs and wants of someone who faces me and that puts an imperative on me and demand on me. And then I began to think—isn't that also true, when I see other species, even plants, if I see a cherry tree that is broken by the wind, for example. I mean, I had this kind of simple statement, that I came upon a couple of years ago, that to see something is to see what it requires to exist. If I see a tree, I also see that it requires earth and sunlight. That's true of anything. If I see an object of furniture, I see that it requires a stable position in order to exist. We do see needs and wants directly. And then to see what it requires is to sense the kind of action that would supply this requirement. For example, if I see a deer, which has been caught in branches in the flooding river, I see that it needs to be freed from these branches or it will drown. And at the same time I see that I could do that. Or somebody could do that, if not me, maybe somebody else. I experience myself as different motor possibilities to rescue something or protect it, or restore, or repair it. That's true just of our ordinary perception. Just when we walk around, what we see are not just shapes and forms and colours. There are distinct and independent beings, that we see what they require. And if we get active, we sense the sorts of actions that could supply their needs. So, I always started from thinking about Levinas's idea that we see the other face as needy and putting demands on us and extending that across nature.

Then, I guess, on the other side, I began thinking more and more about Kant and this idea of ethics being equated with conscious and rational actions. And once I began thinking this way, it seemed to me very clear that we don't admire people who always act out of rationality. I think of some examples from literature, but I can take this example from diving. You know, I went diving in the ocean a number of times. And when you dive, on the board there is a dive master. And every dive master I ever went with, you know, you instinctually trusted. You saw that this is a man who is calm and collected. And if you are in trouble, he will save you. Maybe even at the risk of his own life. And then, you know, sometimes I've gone diving with people that, you know, certainly, not a big contribution to the world, you know, people who are obese and lazy and egotistical and so on. And you see this strong young man would actually risk his life to save this person. And you can ask: Is it rational? I mean, whose life is worth more? But then you realise that the dive master doesn't ask this question, "Is this person worth risking my life to save?" Because he acts instinctually. His bravery is something that we think is in his nature. This is a sort of thought we have. That some people are strong and brave and their acts are with clarity, they see what's to be done at once. I mean, it is like the same person who sees somebody fallen into a river and instinctually jumps into frozen water to save that person.

And then the other example I had is of some women who just simply seem to have a big heart. They're just drawn to caring for children, and caring for animals. I think of some young farmer who I see at the pet store. She has, I don't know, six or seven children, most of them are adopted. But at the same time, every time you see her at the store, you know, there are baby rabbits over here and the birds, and cats, and dogs. She just takes care of everything. She is a person who has a big heart. It's like natural for her to take care of creatures of all size. So, those are the sorts of people we admire and trust. If we have an orphan, we don't want to give it to a woman who's so rational and has to think out rationally the motivations for everything she does. We give to people whose goodness and caring nature is instinctual. There is a lot of that in Nietzsche—the idea that there are noble instincts. And that people who are noble act by instinct. You know, these people are not very intelligent, they are not very calculating in that way. And as a result, sometimes they don't survive so well, because they don't calculate everything. They do generous and noble actions that may, you know, bring risks to themselves and loss to themselves, but this kind of noble generosity is instinctual and not calculating.

JS: Is there a relation to animals here?

AL: Almost every day I walk in the backyard and I see things that just blow my mind. You know, I live with a lot of birds. And you could see out in nature every day how these little birds attack cats and hawks and so on to save their nest. I mean, if you want to understand what is maternal instinct and mother love, you can see it in the very pure form in birds and other species. A lot of the virtues that we admire are virtues that we share with other species. Like generosity and courage and caring.

THE SACRED

JS: Your books and essays often end with the themes of beauty, death, sacrifice, or the sacred. And such themes are articulated in close proximity to the realm of religion. It seems that via Bataille you link the realm of nature and bestiality with that of the sacred. Why do you think it is relevant to reflect on the realms of the sacred or the transcendent? Isn't it because our ethical orientations and highest causes would be impossible to ground without such experiences and encounters?

AL: Considering the last question, I can say that I have not gone in that direction. The thing that was for me so extraordinary in Levinas is that there is an ethical experience. That direct perception of someone facing me is an experience of being obligated. So it is an immediate experience. Yeah, I was profoundly convinced of that.

JS: And how do you distinguish it from just ordinary experiences?

AL: By the fact that I feel obligated. Levinas himself says it—I don't remember where he wrote this, I think, I had some conversations with him—you walk by the street and somebody greets you and you already feel obliged to answer. It's a demand. That's very striking. And I think everybody feels that, I mean, it's a direct experience, it's not some, you know, hypothetical idea.

Speaking about the influences on my understanding of the sacred, I think I was very influenced here by Bataille. I've got from him the idea that the sacred is not only the heavenly, celestial, but is also in the realm of death and corruption, and blood, and sex, and so on. Bataille got it out of anthropology, and that seems to me very true of real religions, religions that have existed in humanity. You know, when I spoke the other night about sacrilege. I feel that the word sacrilege can disappear from modern discourse, even from modern religious discourse, but I think that the sense of sacrilege is very strong, even in non-believers. To the idea that somebody would go in some sacred place and desecrate it, our first reaction is horror. I mean, to see what they did to the Egyptian pharaohs—to put them on display for tourists—it's just shocking. And you don't have to believe in Egyptian religion to be shocked. We sense that there are things that are outside of the profane world, that are not just for use, and calculation and appropriation. And that there is a sort of sense of power in it. At that talk I emphasised this idea that death is power. There are corpses that are sacred in that way. There's power there. There's violence in a corpse. If we just take the word sacred in the etymological sense, "sacrum" in Latin is "separated." It's what is separated from the world of work and reason. I started to think in this way, inspired by Bataille, but then the more I thought of concrete cases, when I had reason to think about certain religious events and so on, it confirmed this thought.

JS: But to you this experience does not work as a motivation for ethical actions? Or does it?

AL: I think it does for a people who have a strong sense of the sacred. To some measure it would, but not in a kind of rationalistic way. You know, people say that we need religion as a kind of guarantee of the seriousness of ethical laws. That I don't think is the case. That seems to me a kind of empty concept of religion. That God is a kind of super policeman. And it seems to me that most people don't seriously believe that anyhow. I mean, the very fact that so many people who don't believe and don't have any religion, who are atheist, are often more irreproachably ethical and moral. We all know many such people. People are generous and truthful, and honest, and so on. And they have no idea that there is a policeman in the sky watching them.

STYLE

JS: I would like to put forward a question concerning your philosophy's style or its form of expression. Your philosophical language is extremely figurative, personal, impressive, emotional, and even passionate. You do not avoid literariness.

AL: I guess I have two thoughts. First of all, I don't like to think about how I write. Because, I think, I write naively. And, you know, if I have something that I want to communicate, sometimes I try it in one way, the other and then I find something that seems to work. But I don't like to think about it. Because it seems to me that if one would think about it too much, one would make it into a kind of recipe. And that's what I want to avoid.

But on the other hand, I discovered this in teaching, in teaching like Heidegger. When I was trying to explain Heidegger to students, I often found that using the resources of the English language and English idiom, you know, I could actually say things that are clearer than Heidegger said. Can you grab this distinction between "existenzial" and "existenziell," or even "ontic" and "ontological"? This is very bad terminology, because "ontological" should mean the logos, the discourse about the ontic. And that's not what he means. He means the dimension of Being and not beings. He chooses these technical words that often aren't very good. Then I discovered that using English, for example, the translation they have of "Zuhandenheit" and "Vorhandenheit"—"readiness to hand" and "presence at hand." That's not English at all. It's a verbal invention. It occurred to me one day—we have the ordinary English expression "within reach." "Within reach" are the things that are available to the hand, and that's the much better term for translation of "Zuhandenheit". I began to think in that way, and I began to see that to really communicate clearly philosophical insights I want to use all the resources of language. And the real masters of language are literary writers. They are the ones who master the vocabulary, and the grammar, and the rhetoric. I got further and further away from technical jargon. And then the other idea I have is very simple—I want to write well. I don't see any virtue in writing bad English, confused, pompous, academic English. So these are very simple ideas.

JS: When giving lectures you use music, photos, and other artistic elements, mixing them together into somewhat a unified performance. You read your texts rhythmically, and it sounds as if you narrate a poem. It seems that you try to create an atmosphere of the ritual. Isn't it?

AL: Yeah, that too. I have a very simple idea—instead of a professor just standing behind the lectern and looking down and turning the pages, I play a little music, just a few minutes before and sometimes after. Because after the talk, usually you invite questions, but sometimes people need a few minutes to come up with a question. I would play a few minutes of music instead. It is things like that, very simple little ideas. So why not have photographs, images that would be helpful? You know, philosophers, of course, have always used images, sometimes as illustrations, but they don't necessarily have to be direct illustration—sometimes an image just gives you a general sense of an atmosphere or a level, or dimension, or a mood. It doesn't really have to be an illustration of something in your philosophical text. A few times I did a kind of complex performance bringing costume and make-up, and images, and music, and it was much more theatrical. But to me it is always hard to know how well they work, because I can't see what the audience sees. I just thought that these things communicate more vividly, more forcefully, sometimes more clearly than just reading the text.

JS: Is it based on your assumption that philosophy can't be expressed fully within the realm of the concept alone?

AL: In a certain way that's true. And a kind of thought I had about it was this: A long time ago I had a colleague that I admired very much. He was very broadly read. He read everything. And he was not dogmatic, and he was open to things. And I was just a young guy at that time. And I was very devoted to Merleau-Ponty. And one day I thought he should read Merleau-Ponty. And I should give him the book. And then I began to think, if I gave him a book, he would read it, because he really read everything. But I thought that he didn't have the kind of sensibility for it. And then you go to philosophy meetings, you see some people have a real Nietzschean sensibility. They perceive and feel, and discern things in a kind of Nietzschean way. And other people have a much more sort of logical and structured sensibility. That time I thought that the reason that some people are very devoted to Merleau-Ponty, or others to Heidegger, or others to Kant is not simply that they are convinced intellectually by certain ideas. But also that a thinker thinks with his or her perceptions and sensibility too. I used to go to these little meetings. There was a Husserl circle, and a Merleau-Ponty circle. And really there were different kinds of people there. And there was a different mood, a different tone of voice—people spoke differently. So in Merleau-Ponty's circle people had a kind of a soft voice, and subtlety. Whereas, in Husserl's circle it was much more black and white. People were different.

THE SENSE OF PHILOSOPHY

JS: It seems that your philosophy is somehow deeply connected with your practice of travelling. You travel to encounter uncultivated nature and often to non-Western regions, countries, places, communities, or persons. Am I right thinking that the aim of such travels, experiences, and encounters is to find an actual alternative to Western modernity, which was criticised by Nietzsche, Heidegger, and others?

AL: Again, my attitude is very simple. I always wanted to see the world. I've never got tired of it. It seems that most people get tired of the world after a while. They don't want to go to Spain or Africa, just stay home. I never get tired of it. When I went to other places, I certainly was interested in the thought of these cultures as much as I could make contact with it. And I more and more respected the thought outside of this Western modern rationality.

Somebody said yesterday that maybe philosophy will come to an end. For Heidegger philosophy is a Greek rationality. He says philosophy is Greek and German. But maybe that will come to an end, at least in your lifetime. In this global world very soon, China will be the biggest economy and the dominant economy in the world. I wouldn't be surprised if this sort of characteristically Greek and German tradition of thinking comes to an end. Right now nothing is happening in philosophy anywhere: in Germany or France, or Scandinavia, or Japan, or in England—nowhere. But I don't think we should see very much in that. Because it seems that in every realm of culture there aren't great thinkers in every generation. For a while it just looked like the West was imposing itself on everything. But now as the West is doing so badly economically, militarily, and so on, the other parts of the world are becoming much more affirmative. It may well be that strands of thought that are leftover from the past—in Africa, in Asia, and so on—will become more important. There was a woman who was applying for the position in ethics at my university. And she pointed to the four most important ethical thinkers. I think they were British names. And she said they were all white males. She was suggesting that the ethics that we have is really constructed for white, male, middle-class academics. But for a long time what I always thought is that, if you read ethics books, it was so many of these examples that are so typically middle class, there are issues that come up only in this prosperous little bourgeois economy. And so it seemed to me that it was said that, if we talk about ethics, we shouldn't talk about the situation of postcolonial Africa and Australian aboriginals, and Native Americans, and so on. So at least it seems to me that in the area of ethics we are beginning to get more diverse and global kinds of thinking. I imagine that in the future philosophy will be much more diverse.

JS: Do you see something that is definitively worth saving in the Western tradition of philosophy, something that is uniquely from European sources?

AL: Certainly. Absolutely. If we look at the bookshelf of the main thinkers of philosophy from ancient Greece to today—it's an astonishing treasury of deep and enlightening thought. So many people outside philosophy feel that. I'm thinking of someone like Feyerabend who often read even ancient and medieval philosophers, because he found there such extraordinary insights. As you know, Einstein was quite interested in Bergson—they had an exchange, and so on. It's a marvellous treasury of thought, this tradition of philosophy. And it seems to me that all of us who have some kind of conversation with people in another field (like in my university sometimes I am an outside reader for a dissertation in some other fields, in psychology, or history, or even in physics), you notice that these people are always terribly interested in what philosophers have to say about it. Because they do find it very striking and often very helpful. It's very precious not only for philosophers but for humanity.

On *Violence and Splendor*

by Graham Harman

Fans of Alphonso Lingis have cause for delight in the recent appearance of his new book *Violence and Splendor*.[1] Lingis is of Lithuanian ancestry but native to the rural region near Chicago, and has been well known since the 1960s in several capacities. In his early career he was known primarily as an encyclopedic authority on French phenomenology, in particular as the key English translator of the philosophers Levinas and Merleau-Ponty. As a professor at Penn State he was a popular and magnetic character, earning the allegiance of generations of students due to an informal personality and a startling mid-block household filled with live tropical birds, sharks, octopi, and electric eels, life-sized wooden Buddhas, flourishing colonies of bees, specimens of colorful moths and beetles, and a bathroom mirrored on all horizontal and vertical surfaces. As an author of books he emerged relatively late, in 1983, with his debut *Excesses: Eros and Culture*.[2] This work set the pattern for his future writings, mixing philosophical erudition with travel narratives from the most exotic locations. Along the way he established a reputation with many readers (including me) as one of the greatest living masters of English prose. Lingis has been retired from Penn State for nearly a decade and now lives near Baltimore, where he continues to write in the same spirit found in his earlier books.

Aside from his running commentary in a recent book of photographs by Mark Cohen,[3] *Violence and Splendor* is the first new book by Lingis to appear since *The First Person Singular* in 2007.[4] Lingis's favored genre is the short or medium-sized chapter. Aside from his 1998 classic *The Imperative*, we rarely find Lingis attempting to systematize the content of his books. Perhaps in keeping with Nietzsche's maxim that "the will to system is a will to falsity," he prefers to maintain the integrity of his individual chapter themes, not yoking them together with any sort of rigid framework. In one respect *Violence and Splendor* takes this preference to a new extreme, offering twenty-five short pieces clustered together in five parts of varying length. Those parts are entitled as follows: Spaces Within Spaces, Snares for the Eye, The Sacred, Violence, Splendor. But in another respect, the new book links its sections loosely through recurring references and proper names, like Wagnerian leitmotifs announcing the occasional reappearance of sword, giant, and Tarnhelm. Not surprisingly, the book is a pleasure to read; it is even a pleasure to gaze upon and leaf through, due to the author's typically enchanting photography. In what follows I will offer samplings from the book by briefly considering one chapter from each of its five sections.

The opening chapter of the book is entitled "Extremes," and is noteworthy for its style no less than its content. Like many high artists, Lingis often reacts with boredom or dismay to technical speculations on the workings of his style. Yet I am obliged to risk his annoyance here by noting his powerful use of second-person narrative, one of the staples of his books. On the very first page of *Violence and Splendor*, we read as follows: "Forty years ago you crossed the Atlantic by ship . . ."; "In Bali you got very sick . . ."; "From Tierra del Fuego you took a ship to Antarctica . . .".[5] No, I did not. But in the hands of Lingis the technique is powerful, forcing the reader into an illusion of direct experience. Of course, this apparently direct experience is mediated through the suggestions and recollections of Lingis himself, who resembles a hypnotist or a Gandalf telling us our fate in reverse. The opening chapter of the book has no "plot" and reaches no conclusion. Instead, it simply draws us from our normal space of daily life and thrusts us into a new geography. While ill with hepatitis in Bali, we have nothing to do but kill several weeks on the seashore, not far from the shark-patrolled Wallace Trench, seven kilometers deep. The Balinese "are not seagoing people,"[6] Lingis says, reminding us of Gibbon's remarks on the terror of the great ocean as felt by the Romans, bound as they were to their little Mediterranean.[7] The Balinese irrigate their crops from the crater lakes of volcanoes, "but at the end of the day" these Balinese "descend to the ocean shore, hundreds of them, and seat themselves on the dunes where they wait, silenced by the descending sun."[8] Your hepatitis is no longer a miserable tourist's setback, but an opportunity to rest side by side on the Balinese seashore with the silent natives descended each evening from their volcanic highland lakes. In the next paragraph you are on a ship to Antarctica. You are not initially in romantic authorial isolation far at sea. Instead, you are surrounded by numerous other tourists, though you soon sequester yourself in your room and gain a reputation as an anti-social. Left alone, "you gaze in silence at the glaciers imperceptibly flowing into the ocean, ice millions of years old, compacted under enormous weight so that the crystalline structure of the ice is changed . . . ."[9] In one sense, nothing at all has happened in this page-and-a-half of an opening chapter. But in another, you may as well have traveled to another planet with these brief introductory words. You have entered the world of Alphonso Lingis, in which the reader shares the most astounding travel experiences with the author, who successfully creates the illusion that no author is present and that everything is unfolding in the reader's own life. There is incredible solitude in this literary world, despite the generosity of the author's descriptions, and despite the lack of elitism in the friendships he has us strike up along the way with slum-dwellers, academics, artists, dentists, and young children.

The title of Chapter 9, "The Fallen Giant," is a phrase normally used metaphorically to describe prominent humans who have undergone an abrupt diminution in social status. But here it is meant literally, and refers to an actually fallen actual giant from the world of plants. As Lingis begins: "The sign does not say when the sequoia fell. Or why. Perhaps it died of old age."[10] We are immediately informed that sequoias have been known to live up to 3,267 years. Counting backwards, this places us in 1256 B.C. as the possible birthdate of a sequoia dying of old age today—born five years prior to Hercules, and dead under Obama, Cameron, and Sarkozy. A flood of numbers quickly follows. The dead sequoia was 220 feet high and 72.6 feet in circumference. Like all numbers, these give us little guidance except by way of comparison, and this is just what Lingis gives us: a blue whale can be up to 110 feet long, and the figure rises to 130 feet for the dinosaur known as *Argentinosaurus huinculensis*. Both of these colossal sentient creatures are eclipsed by the fallen sequoia now lying before us. The author invites us further to imagine the ascent of the tree, its life fully invested in upward ascent, given that many of its branches die along the way. In the manner of Leibniz, Lingis observes that this tree is not a mere aggregate of parts: "the life attached to the enormous inner space of the sequoias, to these hundreds of tons of matter, is somehow one. One life governs the system you see in the branches..."[11] Nonetheless, "each branch has to adjust to local conditions and events," and "the mighty trunk itself... [also] has had to adjust to the impact and pressures of events. Swerves of bark mark these adjustments."[12] But despite these local variations and events, Lingis remains true to the guiding insight of phenomenology concerning the unity of sensuous objects beneath their sparkling contours. For "when this tree died, it died everywhere,"[13] and "the sense of life attached to the enormous inner space of a sequoia, or to that of a beached blue whale, dominates our perception of their surface colors and forms."[14] Elsewhere, our sense of the unified life of "guppies or sandflies . . . overwhelms our fascination with their external designs and colors."[15] The potency of this life is often staggering. Tiny plants of 0.6 millimeters in size, Lingis reports, are able "to produce 1 nonillion (1 with thirty zeroes) new plants in four months, a volume of flowering plants equal to the size of the Earth."[16] These reflections on the inner life of things turn Lingis explicitly to a meditation on the philosophical concept of *substance*, which he has elsewhere tried to revive in a stirring and under-read article on Levinas, printed in an obscure periodical.[17] Modern philosophy "pronounced us incapable of knowing the substance, the nature, or the essence of things."[18] Empiricist philosophy turns appearances into discrete sense data, phenomenology converts them into shifting profiles, and Heidegger into an instrumental layout of practical purposes. But Lingis (with a passing nod to Oliver Sacks) makes the intriguing claim that "the distinction between appearances and things that appear is peculiar to vision and does not really have analogues in the realm of sound, taste, odor, and the tangible."[19] Summarizing Heidegger's distinction between the *zuhanden* and the *vorhanden*, in which entities become visible primarily through malfunction, Lingis asks: "is not this a strangely narrow picture of our experience?"[20] Far from agreeing that substances are inaccessible to human knowledge, Lingis favors a form of what analytic philosophers call "direct realism," in which human insight makes direct contact with the things rather than with mere representations of them: "When we look at the butterflies, trees, and mountains in their independence of and indifference to us, we see them as they are."[21]

Chapter 9, "Sacrilege," begins with a sinister photograph of knives, followed shortly thereafter by sinister words: "In a sacrifice something supremely precious—our finest harvest and livestock, our firstborn son—is set aside from all use, separated from the profane sphere. What is set apart from all profane use is separated absolutely, definitively, in being destroyed."[22] It is in this spirit that we must interpret the two most troubling stories in the book, both of them found in the present chapter. In the first story, the author visits a photography show and passes behind the photos to find a disturbing installation: "a man, powerfully muscled and virile, naked, hanging upside down, his feet bound by a rope looped over a hook in the ceiling."[23] This is a real man, no mannequin. Along the walls are "piles of knives . . . butcher knives, serrated knives, hunting knives,"[24] as if placed there deliberately to incite cruelty against the naked human suspended from the ceiling. Although Lingis remains passive, his companions do not: "Finally one of us took a knife and cut the rope; the man fell to the floor." A student named Andy mutters alarmingly: "The show is not over like that." Andy grabs a knife, stabs at the naked man with full force, but barely succeeds in grazing his body. Instead, the sacrificial animal turns out to be Andy himself, for "he had thrust so violently that, without realizing it or feeling it, his hand had slipped off the handle and down the blade, which cut deeply into the palm of his hand and his fingers."[25] Blood splatters everywhere, as with any sacrifice by knife. Later, surgeons are unable to fully repair the damaged hand, and Andy's career as a musician ("something supremely precious") is ended. Nonetheless, he emerges from this saga "more energized and ebullient than before."[26] Lingis adopts a less passive role in the second story, giving us instead a confession worthy of Augustine or Rousseau. Lingis meets a young boy in Istanbul named Omar, who takes him to the cathedral of Saint George; as a Muslim, the boy prefers to wait outside. Amidst the candles and incense of the empty cathedral, he finds the tombs of the Patriarchs of Orthodox Christendom. Checking carefully to make sure no one is in the cathedral, he opens the heavy lid of one of them; blood rushing to his face, he finds only a bronze coffin. Thwarted by this unexpected obstacle, his temptation to sacrilege might seem to have passed. But much like the Franks cutting down the sacred trees of the Goths,[27] his urge to violate the sacred remains unquenched: "I moved back to the catafalque, lifted the lid again, set it back and lifted the lid of the bronze coffin." The final obstruction to sacrilege now removed, the author witnesses "a dark brown skull showing under what looked like shreds of dried beef, scabs in the eye sockets, and patches of skin shriveled from the crooked rows of the teeth."[28] Leaving the cathedral, he goes off for tea with an unsuspecting young Omar, though "the enormity of what I had done tormented me for days, for weeks."[29] Perhaps what makes the tale so disturbing is that it lacks any of the usual motives to crime (and if discovered in the act, it is as a criminal that he would have been treated). We imagine most crime as motivated by the pursuit of wealth, of sexual violation, or perhaps of revenge. The coffins of Saint George were left relatively unsecured for the simple reason that, unlike gold, no one really aspires to direct commerce with the decayed head of an Orthodox Patriarch. While the author expands his geography beyond the United States to include such regions as Balinese fields beneath volcanic craters, the glaciers of the Antarctic, and the inner lives of sequoias and microbes, he also finds himself tempted to cross the sacred boundary separating us from the sealed-off remains of the dead. But the teahouses of Istanbul do not assuage his conscience, as for once he discovers a space in the world that he wishes he had never entered.

The theme of corpses returns in Chapter 21, "The Art of

War." War has been glorified in the arts from ancient times until relatively recently. "This art depicted the ruler as sublime in himself, absorbing into his destiny the lives of nameless multitudes. It depicted the blood of defeated armies and massacred populations turning into golden radiance about the victorious warlord."[30] Above these corpses stand God or the nation, apportioning mass death by a supreme and glorious decree. The situation changes with Francisco de Goya's series of etchings, *Disasters of War*, first published in 1863, more than half a century after their completion. Goya had experienced the Napoleonic rampage through Spain, and though he was accused of French sympathies himself, that sympathy is not evident in his etchings. "They depict close-up men cornered and disarmed and then castrated and dismembered, the infirm and aged unable to fight or flee [are] butchered, children mutilated and slaughtered."[31] The heroic narratives of war are replaced by an art in which "soldiers, peasants, women and children tear at one another like so many rabid dogs. Goya depicts mutilated corpses covered with flies and picked at by vultures under dark skies, where there is no god above to witness, pity, and redeem so much agony, so many deaths."[32] These depictions of massacre later become an object of massacre themselves, at the hands of the "shock jock" British artists Jake and Dinos Chapman, who serve as recurring characters throughout Lingis's book. "In the year 2000 they purchased for £50,000 a set of Goya's etchings, and painted grinning clown and puppy-dog faces over the faces Goya had depicted stricken with heart-wrenching pathos."[33]

And here we encounter one of the central tensions of *Violence and Splendor*. On the one hand we still find the Lingis of *The Imperative*, for whom it is ethically binding to stamp out a burning cigarette in a forest, and even binding not to abuse the preciousness of such items as rare bottles of wine by consuming them carelessly or under inappropriate circumstances. In the chapter on the sequoia described earlier, when Lingis muses that "perhaps it died of old age," we sense his genuine concern that it might have been knocked down through the perversity of vandals or a lumber company. Everywhere in his writings, Lingis seems concerned that the intrinsic powers of the things themselves should be allowed to shine forth in all their splendor. But *The Imperative* is not really a "normative" book, since there Lingis also admits that there is an indeterminacy related to the existence of an imperative in things. As he wrote in that work, with a gripping cruelty: "We do have the power to crush the penguin chick and knock over the sunflower with a blow, as we may block and muddy the river, but our cruelty and our disdain feel the panic of the chick and the vertical aspiration of the sunflower."[34] In this sense *The Imperative* is more a work of ontology, and counts as a book of ethics only insofar as our ethical subtlety is ripened by the notion of a command emanating from the inner life of things. For the existence of an imperative can also serve to provoke aggression and violation, as in the cases of the naked man hanging from the ceiling of an art gallery, the coffin of an Orthodox Patriarch, humans reduced to mutilated corpses by Napoleonic armies, or the art treasures of Goya defenseless against vandalism by the Chapman Brothers—who would perhaps be interested in crushing the penguin chick, knocking over the sunflower with a blow, and blocking and muddying the river, presumably uttering swear words while doing so. Not only is this ambiguity never resolved by Lingis—it is even the central theme of his book, as seen from the two main words in the title *Violence and Splendor*. But the author limits himself to describing this reversibility rather than attempting to resolve it.

The book ends with Chapter 25, "War and Splendor." This chapter ends the book on a warm note of optimism, with splendor prevailing over violence. It begins with the Rio Carnaval, in which the impoverished slum-dwellers save for years to purchase costumes for an *escola de samba* (samba club). In Carnaval, "everything—plants, insects, birds, beasts, heroes, knaves—becomes beauty, samba, and alegria."[35] The contrast between Lingis's first visit to Carnaval and contemporary world events is explicitly marked: "I arrived the week of the outbreak of the First Gulf War, in which thirty-four advanced countries united in no higher cause than to secure for themselves the sources of cheap petroleum. At the Rio Carnaval, I thought this is the most important event on the planet."[36] The collected writings of Lingis might easily be viewed as a multi-volume account of a global Rio Carnaval, with "the Rio Amazonas and Rio Tocantins, the spectacled bears, the golden lion tamarins, and the toucans, the Indians of the Amazon and the outposts of the Inca, the queens of Africa, the *bandeirantes* (slave hunters and prospectors), the *quilombolas* (escaped slaves), the travelers of outer space."[37] The chapter shifts quickly from the Rio Carnaval to a similar outburst of *alegria* in Papua New Guinea, at the so-called Mount Hagen show (the gorgeous photograph on the book's cover depicts a Mount Hagen celebrant). Although the Papuans were dismissed by Australians as "Stone Age people and savages,"[38] Lingis reports that their wars were primarily theatrical: "When battles did break out, they were so constrained by rules and fought with weapons so ineffective—the arrows without fletching are really inaccurate—that it would be rare that anyone was actually killed."[39] While the First Gulf War prepares industrial mechanisms for slaughter in the name of cheap oil, Lingis finds that war in Papua *is* splendor: "battles were fought without leaders or strategies, each warrior darting and shooting his arrows where he could, exposed to volleys of arrows and spears, exposed not only to cunning and hostile humans but also to supernatural powers and the weapons of sorcery. Battles where no territory was taken, nor women captured or wealth plundered."[40] We are no longer in the world of Goya, and also not in the world of

Jake and Dinos Chapman, despite the author's trace of apparent sympathy for their frank violations of normal limits of artistic behavior. Ultimately, Lingis's real preference is not for crushing the penguin chick, but for splendor in all its historical and animal forms:

> We shall not define with one concept the splendor that glitters and resounds under Mount Hagen, in the liturgical processions in Byzantium and the high mass of Medieval cathedrals, in the Negara, the theater-state of old Bali, in Carnival in Rio de Janeiro—in the plumage and dance of the Great Argus pheasant, in the sun's gold spread over the blue oceans, in the fisherman rowing with golden oars . . . We are mesmerized by beauty as birds-of-paradise are mesmerized by their glittering plumes in their courtship dances; we create beauty as in the primordial ocean mollusks create the iridescent colors and intricate designs of their shells.[41]

In recent philosophy we find no other prose stylist capable of such extended literary brilliance—not even in France, where Merleau-Ponty's finest gemstones tend to be wrapped and muffled in the surrounding cotton of technical argument.

For this reason, it seems appropriate to end this review of Lingis's latest book with the closing half-sentence of the book itself. When observing the festival at Mount Hagen, the second highest volcano in Papua New Guinea: "you feel your blood hot and surging with the exultation of two thousand men and women, of 125 tribes, zigzagging back and forth like slow-motion bolts of lightning across the crowded field of the magnesium-white sun."[42]

[1] Alphonso Lingis, *Violence and Splendor* (Evanston: Northwestern University Press, 2011).
[2] Alphonso Lingis, *Excesses: Eros and Culture* (Albany: SUNY Press, 1983).
[3] Alphonso Lingis, *Wonders Seen in Forsaken Places: On Photography and the Photographs of Mark Cohen* (Chester Perkowski, 2010).
[4] Alphonso Lingis, *The First Person Singular* (Evanston: Northwestern University Press, 2007).
[5] Lingis, *Violence and Splendor*, 5.
[6] Lingis, *Violence and Splendor*.
[7] Edward Gibbon, *History of the Decline and Fall of the Roman Empire*, Vol. 1 (Philadelphia: Birch and Small, 1804), 20.
[8] Lingis, *Violence and Splendor*.
[9] Lingis, *Violence and Splendor*, 6.
[10] Lingis, *Violence and Splendor*, 59.
[11] Lingis, *Violence and Splendor*.
[12] Lingis, *Violence and Splendor*.
[13] Lingis, *Violence and Splendor*.
[14] Lingis, *Violence and Splendor*, 60.
[15] Lingis, *Violence and Splendor*.
[16] Lingis, *Violence and Splendor*.
[17] Alphonso Lingis, "A Phenomenology of Substances," *American Catholic Philosophical Quarterly* 71.4 (1988): 505–522.
[18] Lingis, *Violence and Splendor*, 60.
[19] Lingis, *Violence and Splendor*.
[20] Lingis, *Violence and Splendor*, 61.
[21] Lingis, *Violence and Splendor*.
[22] Lingis, *Violence and Splendor*, 87.
[23] Lingis, *Violence and Splendor*, 88.
[24] Lingis, *Violence and Splendor*.
[25] Lingis, *Violence and Splendor*.
[26] Lingis, *Violence and Splendor*.
[27] Lingis, *Violence and Splendor*, 90.

[28] Lingis, *Violence and Splendor*, 93.
[29] Lingis, *Violence and Splendor*.
[30] Lingis, *Violence and Splendor*, 119.
[31] Lingis, *Violence and Splendor*.
[32] Lingis, *Violence and Splendor*.
[33] Lingis, *Violence and Splendor*, 120.
[34] Lingis, *The Imperative* (Bloomington: Indiana University Press, 1988), 126.
[35] Lingis, *Violence and Splendor*, 139.
[36] Lingis, *Violence and Splendor*, 140.
[37] Lingis, *Violence and Splendor*, 139.
[38] Lingis, *Violence and Splendor*, 141.
[39] Lingis, *Violence and Splendor*.
[40] Lingis, *Violence and Splendor*, 144–145.
[41] Lingis, *Violence and Splendor*, 148.
[42] Lingis, *Violence and Splendor*, 150.

www.ingramcontent.com/pod-product-compliance
Lightning Source LLC
Chambersburg PA
CBHW060835190426
43197CB00040B/2627